# ESSENTIALS OF DISCIPLESHIP

Francis M. Cosgrove, Jr.

NAVPRESS
A MINISTRY OF THE NAVIGATORS
P.O. Box 6000, Colorado Springs, Colorado 80934

The Navigators is an international, evangelical Christian organization. Jesus Christ gave His followers the Great Commission to go and make disciples (Matthew 28:19). The aim of The Navigators is to help fulfill that commission by multiplying laborers for Christ in every nation.

NavPress is the publishing ministry of The Navigators. NavPress publications are tools to help Christians grow. Although publications alone cannot make disciples or change lives, they can help believers learn biblical discipleship, and apply what they learn to their lives and ministries.


Library of Congress Catalog Card Number: 79-93015
ISBN: 0-89109-442-3
14423-395

Second printing, 1980

Unless otherwise identified, Scripture quotations are from the *New International Version*, © 1978 by the New York International Bible Society. Other versions quoted are the *King James Version* (KJV); *The New Testament in Modern English* (PH), © 1958 by J. B. Phillips, published by The Macmillan Company, New York; and the *Revised Standard Version* (RSV), © 1946, 1952, 1972 by the National Council of the Churches of Christ in the U.S.A.

Printed in the United States of America

# CONTENTS

# ILLUSTRATIONS

*Dedicated to those in the body of Christ*
*who have made me a disciple*
*and trained me to be a disciplemaker.*

# AUTHOR

Francis Cosgrove is Director of Church Relations for The Navigators in Colorado Springs, Colorado.

A native of New Orleans, where he met Christ as Savior while in high school, he came in contact with The Navigators while in the Navy. He was ordained into the ministry in 1955 and served as pastor of two small churches in Colorado.

Since joining the Navigator staff in 1955, Francis and his wife Norma have served in a U.S. military ministry in Japan and in military and collegiate ministries in Jacksonville, Florida; San Antonio, Texas; and Charleston, South Carolina. Most recently, they established new ministries in Florida at Fort Lauderdale, Miami, and a nearby Air Force base. While in Florida, the author was also Director of New Life at Coral Ridge Presbyterian Church.

The Cosgroves have two children, Jane and Rodney.

# FOREWORD

There is a little bit of Christopher Columbus in all of us. Many are the people in the 1980s who are like Columbus—dissatisfied with the status quo. Folks looking for new worlds to conquer. Men and women who daily are saying, "There must be more to life than this!"

Francis Cosgrove has put his writing finger and heart on the answer. Discipleship is where the action is. We need to cry like Captain Pinzon of the Nina, "Adelante!" "Onward!" This book is a simple manual for charting some new waters and sailing a course that lands on the shore of discipleship.

But beware! You'll find yourself bucking the tide of the majority of church members who are merely taking a sight-seeing tour. Our day is known for commitment to nothing. The Christian who is committed to nothing in this life knows nothing of the zest of high adventure and the thrill of discipleship discovery.

Nail your colors to the mast. Proudly affirm your loyalty to Jesus Christ as Lord and Captain. Soon you will know why certain people have "a daily, dynamic relationship with God," for you will be one of those people.

Robert D. Foster
Lost Valley Ranch
Sedalia, Colorado

# PREFACE

During his ministry on earth, Jesus Christ inaugurated a bold plan for reaching the world with his gospel. He put into effect a program that would touch every nation with the good news that the Savior had come and that he had died for the sins of men. Early in his ministry Jesus gathered around him a group of followers who were then called disciples. Since he was popular, crowds of people followed him, and on one occasion he expressed to them the terms of discipleship. "And anyone who does not carry his cross and follow me cannot be my disciple. . . . In the same way, any of you who does not give up everything he has cannot be my disciple" (Luke 14:27, 33). Jesus was saying in effect, "If you do not love me enough to do this, there is no way you can be one of my disciples. No way!"

Just before his ascension, Jesus gathered his disciples around him and stated, "All authority in heaven and on earth has been given to me" (Matthew 28:18). Now that was a declaration that should be of tremendous comfort to us, for we need to realize that Jesus Christ has complete authority over everything that goes on in the world. How encouraging it is for us to realize that we are under the authority of the King of kings. Futhermore, we receive directly from him our authority to *do* what he has told us to do. So Jesus told his disciples (as he tells us):

> Therefore go and make disciples of all nations, baptizing them in the name of the Father and of the Son and of the Holy Spirit, and teaching them to obey everything I have commanded you. And surely I will be with you always, to the very end of the age (Matthew 28:19-20).

Making disciples is essential to carrying out the Great Commission, and being a disciple is essential to making disciples.

It is interesting to note that Jesus Christ did not begin his program of reaching the world with perfect people. He began with ordinary people whom he could use, people who had problems, people who were not perfect. In fact, some of them had doubted him.

People that really count today are dedicated, whether it be to Communism or Christianity or another cause. They are disciples. God wants us to be, and to produce, men and women who count because they are dedicated to the cause of Jesus Christ.

Many people may claim to be Christians, but they don't count because they are not truly dedicated to him. When you find a disciple, there is almost no limit to what God can do through that person. All of us should seek to do all we can to be disciples and to make disciples.

How do you recognize a disciple? What are the characteristics of discipleship? More personally, are you a disciple? How can you know that you are one?

That's what this book is all about. We want to examine some essentials of discipleship. Chapters 2-12 examine in detail the essentials of discipleship as they are presented in the profile in Chapter 1.

This book is a sequel to my first book, *Essentials of New Life.* The contents are the outgrowth of my ministry over the years, and became the basis for classes I taught at Coral Ridge Presbyterian Church. *Essentials of Discipleship* comes to you with the prayer that essentials such as lordship, prayer, and servanthood are or will become the basis of your life, just as they have been in the lives of all true disciples since the days of Jesus Christ.

FRANCIS M. COSGROVE, JR.

# CHAPTER 1
# WHAT IS A DISCIPLE?

The last command Jesus gave to his followers was, "Go and make disciples" (Matthew 28:19). Now that's the product we Christians are supposed to produce, and in order to do so we have to be disciples ourselves.

But you might say, "I'm not sure yet whether I am one of his disciples or not." If so, this book is for you, for we want to examine the essentials of discipleship and enable you to see how you are progressing in becoming a disciple for Jesus Christ. A general criterion is to ask if you are involved in any form of evangelism. If you are in any way helping fulfill the Great Commission, then you are involved in making disciples and have to be one yourself.

You might be teaching a Sunday school class or leading a Bible study discussion group. What is your objective in this activity? Is it to help people become disciples of Jesus Christ? Or is it only to help them increase in their knowledge of the Word of God? The latter is certainly necessary, but is that a sufficient objective? Jesus' Great

Commission says that everything we do must be directed toward the goal of making disciples.

When I was ministering with The Navigators in South Carolina, I was responsible for our staff in that state. Early in my responsibility as state director, I met with the seven men I was leading. For four days we discussed this vital question—What is a disciple like? Toward the end of our time together, we came up with eighteen questions by which we could evaluate a person to whom we were ministering.

I used the questionnaire extensively in my ministry, giving it to every person about a year after we had led them to Christ. We wanted them to become involved in reaching their friends for the Savior and then discipling them for him. They were hard questions, but they were not designed to put anyone on the spot. They were written out so that we might evaluate the results of our ministry according to biblical standards. Has this person learned what we have been trying to pass on to him?

Since Scripture does not change, these objectives do not change either. Since South Carolina days I have summarized these eighteen questions in eleven statements, which we may call the biblical profile of a disciple. Please note that a person who sincerely desires to be a disciple will include these characteristics as part of his or her life, but he or she is not limited to just these eleven. Other biblical characteristics will be part of that person's life as well.

The characteristics or essentials of a disciple, which will make up the discussion of Chapters 2-12, are listed on the following two pages with the Scriptures from which they are derived. Each essential will be briefly introduced in this chapter and discussed at length in following chapters.

## A BIBLICAL PROFILE OF A DISCIPLE

1. A disciple is a learner—open and teachable.
—Proverbs 9:8-10; Matthew 4:19; John 6:60-66
2. A disciple puts Christ first in all areas of his life.
—Matthew 6:9-13, 24, 33; Luke 9:23; John 13:13; 2 Corinthians 5:15
3. A disciple is committed to a life of purity and is taking steps to separate from sin.
—1 Corinthians 6:19-20; Ephesians 4:22-5:5; Colossians 3:5-10; 1 Thessalonians 4:3-7; Titus 2:12-14
4. A disciple has a daily devotional time and is developing in his prayer life.
—Psalm 27:4; 42:1-2; Mark 1:35; Luke 11:1-4; 1 Thessalonians 5:17-18; James 1:5-7; 5:16
5. A disciple demonstrates faithfulness and a desire to learn and apply the Word of God through hearing it preached and taught, reading it frequently, Bible study, Scripture memory, and meditation on the Scriptures.
—John 8:31; Acts 2:42; 17:11; Colossians 3:16; 2 Timothy 2:15
6. A disciple has a heart for witnessing, gives his testimony clearly, and presents the gospel regularly with increasing skill.
—Matthew 28:18-20; Acts 1:8; 5:42; 14:21-23; 22:14-15; Romans 1:16; 1 Corinthians 15:3-4; 1 Thessalonians 2:4
7. A disciple attends church regularly to worship God, to have his spiritual needs met, and to make a contribution to the body of believers.
—Psalm 122:1; Acts 16:5; 1 Corinthians 12:12-27; Colossians 1:15-18; Hebrews 10:25

8. A disciple fellowships regularly with other believers, displaying love and unity.
—John 17:22-26; Acts 2:44-47; 4:31-33; Ephesians 4:1-3; Hebrews 10:24; 1 John 1:1-3
9. A disciple demonstrates a servant heart by helping others in practical ways.
—Mark 10:42-45; Acts 6:1-4; 2 Corinthians 12:15; Philippians 2:25-30; 1 Thessalonians 2:8-9
10. A disciple gives regularly and honors God with his finances.
—Haggai 1:6-9; Malachi 3:10-11; 1 Corinthians 16:1-2; 2 Corinthians 8-9; Philemon 14
11. A disciple demonstrates the fruit of the Spirit by an attractive relationship with Christ and his fellowman.
—Acts 16:1-2; 1 Corinthians 13:4-7; Galatians 5:22-23; 1 Peter 2:18-23; 2 Peter 1:5-8

## The Disciple Is a Learner

The man or woman who would follow Christ totally must always be a learner, one who is open and teachable. A disciple realizes that he does not have all the answers. This is a crucial area, for we are in great danger if we think we have nothing more to learn in our Christian life. A disciple of Jesus Christ is always willing to learn something new from someone else. Dawson Trotman used to tell us, "Men, I can learn from a babe in Christ as well as from Christian leaders." A disciple is open and teachable, both by the Lord and other Christians. He is a person who says to others, "I can still be taught and I am willing to learn from you."

Learning sometimes comes through the painful experience of rebuke. During my years of ministry I have seen the lack of a teachable spirit cause great difficulty in many lives. Missionaries sometimes have to be sent home or do not return to the field because they have never learned to take rebuke or instruction from another believer. "The corrections of discipline are the way to life" (Proverbs 6:23).

I am thankful that over the years I have been stiffly rebuked many times by Christian leaders. At times it really hurt, but I was reminded of the words of the writer to the Hebrews: "No discipline seems pleasant at the time, but painful. Later on, however, it produces a harvest of righteousness and peace for those who have been trained by it" (Hebrews 12:11). "Better is open rebuke," said Solomon, "than hidden love" (Proverbs 27:5).

## The Lordship of Jesus Christ

Many passages of Scripture teach the lordship of Jesus Christ, who died for our sins, and purchased our salvation on the cross of Calvary. Since he bought us with a price, he has the right of ownership over us. He has the right to do whatever he wants with that which belongs to him. Because we are his, we are to live for him (see 2 Corinthians 5:15). If we want to be his disciples, we must allow him to be Lord over our life.

Jesus exhorted his followers to seek the kingdom of God first. That is where the battle zone is, for practicing the lordship of Christ is one of the greatest struggles in a Christian's life. It always will be, for it is the battle between self and the will of God. If as a Christian you are having problems, the root cause may be a failure to yield to the lordship of Jesus Christ.

Jesus clearly said that he is Lord of our life (see John 13:13). In context that is a most interesting statement, for he said it after he had washed his disciples' feet. His lordship is one of servanthood, but he is still Lord.

Christ is present in every Christian, everyone who has received him as Savior. But he is truly prominent in some believers, and preeminently supreme in only a few. Which group are you in? Are you putting Jesus Christ first in all areas of your life? If you are, you have made the first step toward being a disciple of the Lord.

## Purity of Life

Many of the practical sections of Paul's letters deal with living a pure life (see Ephesians 4:22-5:5, Colossians 3:5-10, and 1 Thessalonians 4:3-7). These passages challenge us to godliness and righteous living. We are to put off certain impure characteristics and habits and put on those which are pure. When we look at all these teachings, we find definite steps we should be taking to separate from sin.

In a world of sin and corruption, a godly life stands out clearly. It is not an option but a vital necessity. It is one of the means by which we witness to the reality of Jesus Christ in our life, for we do not behave as the world does, nor do we practice evil as the world does.

## Devotions and Prayer

The disciple needs a regular time each day to read God's word, meditate over it, and decide how best to apply it. In addition to regular devotions, the disciple develops in his prayer life. We use the word *develop* because we don't become mature in prayer overnight; it takes time. Bob Foster, a Christian businessman from Colorado, once said that "prayer is the voice of your life. Where you are spiritually is revealed in how you pray." Now think about that a moment. When I pray, I am revealing the extent of my spiritual growth. It is always intriguing to hear a godly man pray, for he obviously has intimate contact with God. He prays out of the experiences of his life and out of his walk with the Lord Jesus.

Many passages of Scripture give us examples of godly men, including Jesus, who had regular times with God. The Psalms are full of expressions of David and other psalmists who considered their times with God absolutely vital.

## The Importance of the Bible

A disciple is committed to the faithful intake of Scripture through hearing, reading, study, memory, and meditation. *Faithful* in this context means "consistent." I thank God for those who early in my Christian life emphasized the importance of studying the word of God consistently. I committed myself to Bible study at least forty-five weeks per year, allowing for a break every now and then. By the grace of God, I've been able to maintain that practice for over twenty years.

How many Christians do you know whose only intake of the Word of God is a weekly diet of listening? They go to church and Sunday school, but all they do is sit and listen. They never take a pencil or pen and write down something they've heard that strikes them, nor do they ever dig into the Scriptures for themselves. A true disciple demonstrates faithfulness and a desire to learn and apply the word of God through regular Bible study.

At one time in his ministry Jesus declared to those who believed in him, "If ye continue in my word, then are ye my disciples indeed" (John 8:31 KJV). The key word in that statement is *continue*. It means to practice and obey God's word every day. It also means regularity in hearing, reading, studying, memorizing, and meditating on it. Jesus said that if we do this, then we are obviously his disciples.

## The Primacy of Evangelism

Christians cannot claim to be disciples unless they are committed to the primary importance of witness and evangelism. A disciple must know how to give his or her testimony. The personal testimony is simply telling what our life was like before we met Jesus Christ and what it is like now. Besides our testimony, we must also know how to present the gospel intelligently. Many opportunities for training in evangelism are available today. One of the best is Evangelism Explosion.[1]

A disciple of Jesus Christ must be committed to sharing his or her faith with others. Are you concerned about the salvation of your friends and relatives? Are you able to give your testimony effectively? Are you learning the gospel? If you are a disciple, then the answer to all of these questions will be yes.

Dawson Trotman, founder and first president of The Navigators, was committed to evangelism. As a Christian he had a passion for sharing the gospel with people who did not know the Savior. When he died at the age of 50, Billy Graham said of Dawson at his funeral, "I think he touched more lives than any man I have ever known."

## THE CHURCH AND BODY LIFE

When you study the history of the early Church in Acts, you find that as men and women came to the Savior, they immediately banded themselves together in small groups to form churches. They worshiped God and used the local assemblies as bases from which to evangelize the regions around them.

In every area in which Paul preached and had results, a church was established. We see this on his first missionary journey. Paul preached the gospel as he traveled through southern Galatia (see Acts 14:2, for example). The first objective he and his team had was evangelism—the proclamation of the good news.

The second objective Paul had was follow-up. After having evangelized the region of southern Galatia, he and Barnabas returned to the cities they had previously visited. There they had a ministry of "strengthening the disciples and encouraging them to remain true to the faith" (Acts 14:22). Paul and Barnabas helped their earlier converts become disciples.

Paul's third objective was church planting. In each group of believers he and Barnabas "appointed elders for them in each church and, with prayer and fasting, committed them to the Lord in whom they had put their trust" (Acts 14:23). Paul and Barnabas planted churches by appointing responsible leaders in each congregation, who were to take care of the spiritual needs of the people.

To attend church is to be part of a local assembly of believers, which is the local manifestation of the body of Christ universal. The writer to the Hebrews warned his generation about forsaking the gathering together of the church of Jesus Christ (see Hebrews 10:24-25). People already had the idea that they did not have to go to church. But Christian fellowship is part of God's plan. He wants his people to gather together to worship him and to strengthen one another.

## Christian Fellowship

Closely associated with the preceding essential is the necessity that every disciple maintain fellowship with other believers. All Christians are called on to associate with other believers and show unity with them whether they belong to the same local church or not.

Every believer should seek regular fellowship with other believers (see 1 John 1:3). Included in this fellowship should be the commitment to work for the visible unity of all believers, not in some organization, but in true brotherly oneness. Paul told us to "make every effort to keep the unity of the Spirit through the bond of peace" (Ephesians 4:3). In other words, each one of us has the responsibility to work at maintaining the unity of the Spirit.

Now the body of Christ already has an eternal spiritual unity that can never be destroyed, but daily unity requires daily effort. Each one of us has to make sure that we are working at maintaining that unity. The psalmist of old exulted when he observed believers living together in unity (see Psalm 133:1). Wherever unity exists, the cause of Christ moves forward.

## The Disciple Is a Servant

Another essential of a disciple's life is serving others. Servanthood was a major characteristic of Jesus' ministry. On one occasion he stated that he had come to serve others by giving his life as a ransom for many (see Mark 10:45).

As I have observed many Christians' lives, this seems to be an area of great weakness in them. Even though Jesus set an example for us, human nature wants to be served rather than to serve.

The Bible outlines the characteristics of a servant of God, by statement and example. We find such things as availability and a humble attitude. The best example is that of Jesus. The true Christian leader is the man or woman who is willing to serve those whom he or she leads.

## The Ministry of Giving

Another essential area of discipleship is that of giving. A disciple must be giving to the Lord's work. Two to three months after someone in my ministry has come to Christ, I sit down with him and share some instruction from the word of God about our responsibility of honoring God with our money. The Bible has quite a bit to say about the subject in both testaments.

In the Old Testament God required a tithe, or ten percent, from his people. But there is an interesting statement that follows that requirement. God also said, "I will rebuke the devourer for your sakes, and he shall not destroy the fruits of your ground" (Malachi 3:11, KJV). Now what is a "devourer"? I believe it is anything that takes your money away from you unnecessarily. The devourer makes the transmission fall out of your car, or the air conditioner burn out at home. I think that the devourer is Satan, the enemy of God and his people. When we do not honor God with our money, we may be letting Satan use it.

Since we obviously do not give to God directly, to whom do we give? Again the Bible gives us some principles, such as Galatians 6:6. "The man under Christian instruction should be willing to contribute to the livelihood of his instructor" (PH).

## The Fruit of the Spirit

The last of the essentials of discipleship discussed in this book is the need for demonstrating the fruit of the Spirit. Paul wrote that "the fruit of the Spirit is love, joy, peace, patience, kindness, goodness, faithfulness, gentleness and self-control" (Galatians 5:22-23). These qualities are the outgrowth of our personal relationship with Jesus and the inner working of the Holy Spirit in our life.

A disciple will attract other people to the Savior if these qualities are seen in his life by all with whom he comes in contact. The person who demonstrates them demonstrates that he or she is Jesus' disciple.

We are to make every effort to develop and demonstrate these qualities, for they do not come automatically. We need to pray, "Lord, I want these characteristics in my life for your sake!" When we have that attitude, the Holy Spirit becomes our helper. The promise is that we will be effective and productive (see 2 Peter 1:8). And that is the goal: as disciples of the Lord Jesus Christ, we will attract others to the Savior by the way our life looks.

---

NOTES: 1. Information on clinics and materials may be obtained by writing Evangelism Explosion III International, P.O. Box 23820, Fort Lauderdale, Florida, 33307.

# CHAPTER 2
# THE DISCIPLE IS A LEARNER

*A disciple is a learner—open and teachable.*

When you look up the word *disciple* in a dictionary, you find that its basic meaning is "a follower of." Another meaning or synonym for *disciple* is *learner*. The original, or secular, word carries with it the idea of apprenticeship, similar to an apprentice in a trade like carpentry. Jesus introduced an added dimension and goal of discipleship in the lives of those who were learning of him. In Luke 6:40 he said, "A student is not above his teacher, but everyone who is fully trained will be like his teacher." When fully discipled, his followers were to be like him, despite their diverse and at times irreconcilable individuality.

The disciple in Christianity is a follower of Jesus Christ, desiring to learn his ways and apply them to his life. This means that a disciple has to be open and teachable. He is a follower who desires to learn.

Being a learner involves perceiving concepts, building principles in our life, and acquiring knowledge. We learn skills as well, in activities such as evangelism, leading a Bible study, or teaching a Sunday school class.

As followers what we learn is more often caught rather than taught. We see something positive in another person's life and we build it into our own life.

Paul told the Philippians to put into practice what they had learned from him through observation (see Philippians 4:9). Paul not only communicated with what he taught, but he was a model to the Philippians in what he did. Paul reminded another church: "You became imitators of us and of the Lord; in spite of severe suffering, you welcomed the message with the joy given by the Holy Spirit. And so you became a model to all the believers in Macedonia and Achaia" (1 Thessalonians 1:6-7). They imitated the model they had been given—the Apostle Paul—and in turn became models to other believers in the two provinces. We have to be sure that the model we follow is Jesus Christ, even as Paul did. "Follow my example, as I follow the example of Christ" (1 Corinthians 11:1).

The Christian disciple must be both a learner of biblical truth and a visible follower of Jesus Christ. That unbeatable combination makes a great impact on others.

## Areas of Life in Which to Develop

We want to discuss four areas of life in which a disciple needs to develop by following Jesus Christ and learning biblical truth. Here are four qualities that he needs to learn and build into his life.

### *Character*

The first area in which a disciple must develop is his character. Men and women of genuine Christ-honoring character are very few. But they are desperately needed if we are to produce other men and women who will represent Christ to the world properly.

Biblically, a disciple is a marked person. If a disciple is functioning as he should, Jesus said that men would recognize them as his disciples (see John 13:35). Do people around you know that you are a disciple of Jesus Christ? The Bible says that as disciples we are to reflect like mirrors the glory of the Lord. Paul wrote, "And we, who with unveiled faces all reflect the Lord's glory, are being transformed into his likeness with ever-increasing glory, which comes from the Lord, who is the Spirit" (2 Corinthians 3:18).

Character forms the inner man out of which flows the man who is visible to the world. In a Christian, character qualities are basically those Christlike qualities that are the fruit of the Spirit living in us: "love, joy, peace, patience, kindness, goodness, faithfulness, gentleness and self-control" (Galatians 5:22-23). These qualities are what people will remember us by.

People should see our love, our joy in the Lord, our peace—the fact that nothing seems to destroy the tranquility of our vital relationship with Christ; our longsuffering when we bear the pressures of life as God would have us. When we demonstrate kindness and goodness toward others as we would the Lord, then our inner character stands out for all to see.

People should see our faith, which is our confidence in God's trustworthiness and promises; our meekness, which is our recognition that God alone is our defense and capable of handling any mistreatment by others; and our self-control.

We must take personal responsibility for character development that is Christlike. Paul wrote to Timothy:

> In a large house there are articles not only of gold and silver, but also of wood and clay; some are for noble purposes and some for ignoble. If a man cleanses himself from the latter, he will be an instrument for noble purposes, made holy, useful to the Master and prepared to do any good work (2 Timothy 2:20-21).

We must take responsibility to become an instrument for noble purposes prepared to do any good work God requires of us.

Solomon made an interesting comment on character: "As dead flies give perfume a bad smell, so a little folly outweighs wisdom and honor" (Ecclesiastes 10:1). A little sin in our life outweighs all that is wise and honorable in our character.

I remember an expression that was used about men whose characters were marred by some small besetting sins: "Slightly soiled; greatly reduced in price!" It was used originally in department store sales of damaged clothing, but it was a tag that stuck to some men because their character was not what it should have been. There were small but visible imperfections.

The disciple as a learner and follower must have a commitment to develop his character so it will reflect Jesus Christ.

*Proficiency in the Ministry*

The second area that a disciple must develop in is proficiency in the ministry. We have learned that the quality of a person's character will be reflected in his or her ministry. If a person is mature in character, he will have an effective ministry; if he is immature or there are weaknesses in his character, he will not have much of a ministry. This is why in The Navigators we concentrate on character development when young men and women come to us for training.

The key to proficiency is a commitment to excellence. Proficiency was a characteristic of the ministry of the Lord Jesus. "People were overwhelmed with amazement. 'He has done everything well,' they said" (Mark 7:37). As a follower of Jesus Christ, we must try to do everything well.

While I served at Coral Ridge, I was always impressed with Jim Kennedy's preaching. His messages were excellent and he ministered to many through them. The quality of his messages caused scores of people to come to a saving knowledge of Jesus Christ. Jim could have sloughed off his responsibility with good excuses about other responsibilities, but he was committed to proficiency in the ministry and took much time to prepare his sermons.

The Christian must strive for the goal of proficiency in the ministry. John W. Gardner has stated:

> We fall into error of thinking that happiness necessarily involves ease, diversion, tranquility, a state in which all of one's wishes are satisfied. For most people, happiness is not to be found in this vegetative state *but in striving toward meaningful goals*.[1]

Everyone of us who would be Christ's disciple must strive for the development of the ministry skills with which God has equipped us. We need to be proficient in the spiritual gifts God has given and carry out our responsibility well. If we concentrate on the quality of our life, it will eventually produce quantity; there will be great fruitfulness. When we in The Navigators look for someone to train in the principles of spiritual multiplication, we look for a person who has demonstrated many of the qualities that are necessary for spiritual reproduction.

Paul says an interesting thing in his letter to the Corinthians:

> Now when I went to Troas to preach the gospel of Christ and found that the Lord had opened a door for me, I still had no peace of mind, because I did not find my brother Titus there. So I said good-by to them and went on to Macedonia (2 Corinthians 2:12-13).

Paul left a promising ministry to go and look for Titus. Why would he give up the opportunity to reach a whole city for Christ to go search for one man? Because Titus was more important to Paul than Troas. Paul knew very well that with proper training Titus would become proficient in the ministry and multiply believers many times over. Paul could reach many more cities with the gospel than just Troas if he had the right man. And Titus was the right man, for quality begets quantity.

When we were ministering in Miami, a high school senior, Jose Ortega, began attending our Bible study. Only a babe in Christ, his commitment to Jesus was crystal clear. I saw in that young man tremendous potential to be developed.

During our study together he answered questions beautifully, for he was well prepared. He participated in the discussion and asked his own incisive questions. He made statements that I had previously heard only from people who had been Christians for several years. He was the kind of man I gave additional time to because I could see what he would be five years down the road.

Quality should be visible in every facet of our ministry. When we realize that whatever we are presently doing is for Jesus Christ, then we will be more concerned about quality that is visible to others.

Dawson Trotman felt so strongly about proficiency in the ministry that he would not allow letters that had typing errors in them or envelopes that were improperly addressed to leave the office. These may have been little details, considered insignificant by some of his critics, but many men and women were trained to produce quality, and consequently made a tremendous impact on the world.

While visiting a Navigator rally in another city one time, I noticed that some of the group were sloppily dressed. This greatly disturbed me, for I knew that eventually this image would be projected to the world at large and would cause some people never to come again. I encouraged the leaders of the rally to emphasize quality, not only in the way the meeting was conducted, but also in the matter of personal dress. Appearance is one aspect of our ministry that should not be overlooked.

If we would exalt Jesus Christ, we must be willing to pay the price for quality. The cost may be high, but the results are tremendous. Development of proficiency in the ministry is a must for a disciple of Jesus Christ.

*Conviction*

There comes a time in our life when it is no longer valid for us to base what we believe on the convictions of others. We must develop convictions that are our own.

We find an excellent example of that in the life of Moses. "By faith Moses, when he had grown up, refused to be known as the son of Pharoah's daughter. He chose to be mistreated along with the people of God rather than to enjoy the pleasures of sin for a short time" (Hebrews 11:24-25). Moses came to the place where the convictions he had learned from his parents had to become his own or had to be abandoned.

When I was ministering in Charleston, South Carolina, part of my work was at The Citadel, a military school similar to West Point. I would visit men in their dormitories and find everything in tip-top condition. Beds were so well made that a quarter would bounce high off the blankets. Everything was neatly in place in the closets. Shoes were shined, uniforms were neatly pressed, and books on the desks were perfectly aligned. It was a beautiful sight, sure to pass the rigorous inspections that were held periodically.

During summer vacation some of the men lived in an apartment owned by the same landlord we had. He complained to me that the Citadel men were quite messy. Why such a discrepancy? The answer is simple. When the men were living in the dormitories, they were required to abide by the regulations. But they had no personal convictions about keeping their place of residence neat. The requirements of The Citadel had never become their own convictions and the men simply did not care enough about the appearance of their apartment to keep it clean.

Personal convictions for the Christian are very important. For the sake of his testimony they are vital in seemingly mundane things like keeping his room clean. A Christian must stand out as being different from the world.

Convictions are also vital in the more spiritual aspects of our life. If we have convictions about being disciples and making disciples, then we will both be and make disciples. If we do not have convictions in this area, then we will neither be nor make disciples. The same is true concerning Bible study. Many people begin studying the Scriptures. In some cases they start because of a challenge or because their friends are doing it. But because they do not have personal convictions about the importance of Bible study, eventually they drop out.

If a person has convictions, he will find the necessary methods to apply them. On the other hand, give a person all the methodology available in the world, but if he does not have convictions, he won't use the methods. Jesus Christ did not give us many details about how the Great Commission was to be carried out. He simply told us to do it. Because he told us to do it, we should have strong convictions about its importance and develop effective methods.

Jim Kennedy, founder of Evangelism Explosion, is a man who is convinced that disciples must learn how to communicate their faith adequately. That conviction came first, and the method came later. Jim eventually developed a workable program that could be used to train laymen in evangelism. Today that method is being used successfully around the world.

*Perspective*

The last major area in his life that a disciple needs to develop is perspective, the ability to see the probable end as well as the beginning. Some people call it bifocal vision, which is the ability to see what is directly in front of you as well as what is down the road in the distance.

Perspective is a rare commodity among Christians. We seem to have the flaw of only seeing the now, the immediate. We are not able to see what the long-range results of our actions might be.

I remember being in a businessman's office once. I was impressed by a sign he had on his desk which read, "How will this pay off five years from now?" Now that's perspective. We need to ask ourself whether what we are doing today will pay off in a desirable way five years from now. A right perspective might cause one to pray something like this: "Lord, if you let me live in this city for five years, allow me to leave behind some people who have met Christ because of my witness and who have been discipled."

Perspective is also an ability to see the things of life from God's point of view, or at least remember that his point of view is different, and clearer, than ours.

Perspective includes a positive view of our immediate circumstances. How do you view circumstances? You can see them as hindrances or as stepping stones. You can view them as defeats or delightful opportunities. The person who has perspective will view all the circumstances of life as stepping stones to better things and as the delightful opportunities of life. He will always be looking down the road, not seeing just the present but the future as well.

How do we build conviction and perspective into our life? Three guidelines apply equally to our own life as well as the lives of others.

*Major on principles rather than methods.* The person who is more concerned about methods of evangelism or follow-up, rather than the necessity of evangelism or follow-up will never do either one. If he does get started, he will fizzle out in a short time. The person with conviction and perspective uses whatever methods are available to him and gets the job done. Since principles are universal, they will work anywhere, at any time. But methods may have to vary from place to place, or time to time.

*Focus on the "why" of what you are doing.* Emphasize the purpose rather than the skills. It is the purpose that will develop the skills. When we know *why* we are doing something, then it is easier to do what we are supposed to do. It is certainly important to learn the skill of evangelism, but unless we know why we should be evangelizing, the skill may remain unused.

The whole Evangelism Explosion program is based on

purpose; the trainees are told why they are doing what they are doing. In the clinics, trainees learn outlines and communicative tools, but the emphasis is on purpose.

*Concentrate on trusting God rather than learning theories about him.* Who do you think knew more about God, Abraham or some of the modern theologians? Abraham may not have known all the ins and outs of theological systems as we know them today, but he certainly knew God intimately and walked with him in submission and obedience.

It is far more important to have a dynamic personal relationship with God than to know and understand every theological detail. A disciple has to learn how to trust God totally. This means walking by faith. It is this firm trust in God that will develop convictions and perspective experience by experience.

Some people have theories about God and walking by faith, but they need to experience it practically. The disciple must learn how to trust God. We may not become giants of faith immediately, but neither did Abraham. We learn to walk by faith just like a child learns to walk physically. The Christian disciple begins with the first step of faith. Then he may fall, but he tries again. And as he persists in trusting God, he learns how to walk by faith.

In a Bible study discussion, a couple shared their struggle with a decision of whether or not they should put their children in a Christian school. They shared how they were evaluating whether they could afford to do so. I saw in them a young couple who were just about ready to take a step of faith. I told them, "First, you must determine what is the will of God for your children. Does he or does he not want you to place your children in this school?" That was the critical issue for them—the will of God for their lives. Once they determined that, the question of finances would be an opportunity to trust God for his provision.

Jesus Christ said, "But seek first his kingdom and his righteousness, and all these things will be given to you as well" (Matthew 6:33). The Lord is saying that we are to concentrate on trusting God and he will provide. This is the major principle of living by faith.

Involved in this is a high view of God and his ability to provide for all of our needs. This is what Scripture says of Abraham: "He did not waver through unbelief regarding the promise of God, but was strengthened in his faith and gave glory to God, being fully persuaded that God had power to do what he had promised" (Romans 4:20-21).

* * *

A disciple, then, is a follower and a learner committed to developing his character and growing more Christlike. When we are willing to learn, we emerge as trophies of his grace and products of his tender, loving care. What an honor it is to be called a disciple of Jesus Christ.

---

NOTE: 1. John W. Gardner, *Excellence: Can We Be Equal and Excellent Too?* (New York: Harper and Row, Publishers, Perennial Library Edition, 1971), p. 178.

CHAPTER

# 3

# THE LORDSHIP OF JESUS CHRIST

*A disciple puts Jesus Christ first in all areas of his life.*

The lordship of Christ is the daily submission and surrender of our entire self to the authority and leadership of Jesus Christ, recognizing his sovereign right to rule preeminently over us. The acknowledgment of Christ's lordship is the abdication of self from the throne of our life and the enthronement of Jesus in self's place.

The lordship of Jesus Christ in a believer's life is the most crucial issue in Christian living. It is absolutely necessary and foundational to Christian discipleship. In fact, this major doctrine of Christianity determines how useful a person will be to God.

All of our aspirations, blessings, and joys of the Christian life are absolutely dependent on our submission to Jesus Christ as Lord of our life. We cannot experience the fullest in Christian living until we commit ourselves unreservedly to the lordship of Christ.

Furthermore, submission to Christ's lordship is not a

one-time experience. We must make Jesus Christ Lord of our life by decision, but we must also follow up that decision with daily recommitment. Every day we must say "Father, I recommit my life to Jesus as Lord!"

## Jesus Christ as Lord

By virtue of the fact that Jesus Christ is God, he already has authority over creation.

### *Who God Is*

The Bible uses many different words and concepts to describe God; these are not just theological terms but facts about God that vitally concern all of us. In order to acknowledge him as Lord practically, we have to know what he is like. Scripture tells us that God is eternal, all-powerful, all-knowing, present everywhere, great, majestic, and glorious. Yet all of these words together fail to describe him fully.

King David, after a life of serving God cried out:

> Yours, O Lord, is the greatness and the power and the glory and the majesty and the splendor, for everything in heaven and earth is yours. Yours, O Lord, is the kingdom; you are exalted as head over all. Wealth and honor come from you; you are the ruler of all things. In your hands are strength and power to exalt and give strength to all. Now, our God, we give you thanks, and praise your glorious name (1 Chronicles 29:11-13).

Not only is Jesus Christ Lord because he is God, but he is also Lord by virtue of the salvation that he secured for us. We cannot save ourselves; there is simply no way we could do it. He alone has provided the redemption necessary for us to have eternal life with him. And because he has, he must be Lord of all. His exalted position and his work are at the heart of the issue of lordship.

*Areas Where Jesus Christ Is Already Lord*

The Bible speaks clearly of a number of areas where Jesus Christ is Lord in practice.

*Jesus Christ is Lord over the angels.* Jesus Christ, the Savior of the world, is superior to the angels: "So he became as much superior to the angels as the name he has inherited is superior to theirs" (Hebrews 1:4). We see this clearly in the Old Testament where the Trinity—God the Father, God the Son, and God the Holy Spirit—is worshiped by the angels, or seraphs. Jesus Christ dazzles the angels of heaven with his glory, and they cry out, "Holy, holy, holy is the Lord Almighty" (see Isaiah 6:1-4).

John saw Jesus as the Lamb of God being worshiped by the uncountable hosts of heaven:

> Then I looked and heard the voice of many angels, numbering thousands upon thousands, and ten thousand times ten thousand. They encircled the throne and the living creatures and the elders. In a loud voice they sang: 'Worthy is the Lamb, who was slain, to receive power and wealth and wisdom and strength and honor and glory and praise!' (Revelation 5:11-12).

*Jesus Christ is Lord over Satan.* Jesus Christ triumphed over Satan in his magnificent victory on the cross of Calvary. The devil is a defeated foe. Paul wrote, "And having disarmed the powers and authorities, he made a public spectacle of them, triumphing over them by the cross" (Colossians 2:15). Jesus Christ is the absolute victor over sin, death, hell, and Satan.

Not only that, but he leads his followers day by day from one victory over Satan to another, if we submit to his lordship. We can be victorious over every temptation: "No temptation has seized you except what is common to man. And God is faithful; he will not let you be tempted beyond what you can bear. But when you are tempted, he will also provide a way out so that you can stand up under it" (1 Corinthians 10:13). Paul states, "If God is for us, who can be against us? . . . No, in all these things we are more than conquerors through him who loved us" (Romans 8:31, 37). We are victorious in and through Jesus.

*Jesus Christ is Lord over the nations.* The nations of the world are under Jesus' control. Pharaoh discovered this when he tried to keep God's people slaves in Egypt. God told him, "But I have raised you up for this very purpose, that I might show you my power and that my name might be proclaimed in all the earth" (Exodus 9:16). The king of Babylon, Nebuchadnezzar, declared, "All the peoples of the earth are regarded as nothing. He does as he pleases with the powers of heaven and the peoples of the earth. No one can hold back his hand or say to him: 'What have you done?'" (Daniel 4:35)

Final authority over the world does not reside in Jerusalem or Cairo, nor Paris or London, nor even Washington or Moscow. The final authority is in the hands of God and in the hands of his Christ. He is the Lord over the nations of the world.

*Jesus Christ is Lord over all creation.* In a magnificent passage on the supremacy of Jesus, Paul stated:

> He is the image of the invisible God, the firstborn over all creation. For by him all things were created:

> things in heaven and on earth, visible and invisible, whether thrones or powers or rulers or authorities; all things were created by him and for him. He is before all things, and in him all things hold together. (Colossians 1:15-17).

Everything visible and invisible was created by Jesus Christ and is sustained by him. In one shovelful of dirt are thousands of forms of life, all created by Jesus Christ. Beyond our earth are millions of galaxies and billions of stars. All of these were made by Jesus Christ. We cannot even begin to fathom inner space with its atoms, electrons, protons, and neutrons that are all whirling around at tremendous rates of speed, but the Bible says that Jesus Christ made them all. Every thing made is subject to the lordship of Christ but one. The only one that is not is man!

*Daily Lordship.* Christians may acknowledge Jesus as Savior and Lord with their lips, yet so few live with Jesus Christ the Lord of their daily lives. Tragically, when Christians do not acknowledge Christ's lordship, they leave behind ruined lives of mediocrity and uselessness.

We have countless examples of God's anger with Christians who do not submit to Christ's lordship. The prophetic books of the Old Testament (Isaiah—Malachi) show God's anger toward his people because they did not respond to his lordship. If God were not angry with man's rebellion, he would not be consistent with his holiness, righteousness, and justice. God's judgment—not unto condemnation—will come on Christians, for Paul declared, "For we must all appear before the judgment seat of Christ, that each one may receive what is due him for the things done while in the body, whether good or bad" (2 Corinthians 5:10). His judgment will be affected by whether or not we have submitted to the lordship of Christ.

Isn't that somewhat harsh of God? Not at all, for just as we do not set conditions for salvation—it is God's salvation—so we can rest assured that we cannot negotiate the terms of lordship. He *is* Lord, and that is not negotiable.

Multitudes of people appear willing to come to Christ and turn over their troubled, ruined lives to him, but they hesitate to turn over their remade lives to him. Some say, "You mean God wants me to be a puppet in his hands? Never!" Many want him as Savior but not as Lord.

## Jesus Christ's Plan for His Disciples

Jesus Christ, because he is Lord, has a plan for each of his children. In submitting to his lordship, we realize his plan for our life.

### *Submission at All Times*

God's plan for us is to be like Jesus Christ. And when we think of his life, we realize that he was totally submissive to the father. Jesus said that his whole purpose in life was "to do the will of him who sent me and to finish his work" (John 4:34). And that's what God asks of us.

If we are to be like Jesus Christ, then we must be submissive to him at all times. "For those God foreknew he also predestined to be conformed to the likeness of his Son" (Romans 8:29). Is it possible for us practically to do this?

None of us can stand before God and say that we have always done things that please him. Our problem is centered in the heart where self-will still struggles with the lordship decision. Frequently it is easier for us to do something that is not in the will of God than to do his will. But God has promised us the power to overcome self and to be submissive to his lordship (see Romans 6). Since his plan is for us to become like Jesus, he will help us reach this goal.

*Submission of Every Area of Our Life*

The struggle of submitting to God in various areas of our life is quite evident. In fact, it is a constant struggle. Much of my counseling has had to do with submission. If only people would submit to God, then a particular problem area could be settled. But people do not want to submit to the Lord, so the problems persist.

J. Oswald Sanders, a missionary leader and statesman, has written:

> A clear and definite activity of the will is involved in recognizing his lordship, since he is to be Lord of all. By her "I will" at the marriage altar, the bride ideally forever enthrones her groom in her affections. In subsequent years she lives out in detail all that was implied in that momentary act of the will. A similar enthronement of Christ can result from a similar act of the will, for the same decision that enthrones Christ automatically dethrones self.[1]

The whole principle of lordship is the abdication of self on the throne of one's life, and the invitation to Jesus Christ to sit on the throne.

The Pie Illustration (Figure 1) communicates the issue of the lordship of Christ. Each segment of the "pie" represents a major area of our life where there is often a struggle over who will control it—self or Jesus Christ. For each of these areas ask the question, Is Jesus Christ Lord? What about possessions? Do they belong to you or to the Lord? After all, he has entrusted them into your keeping and stewardship. What about your plans for the future? Do you seek God's will on what to do or are you just asking God to rubber-stamp what you have already planned?

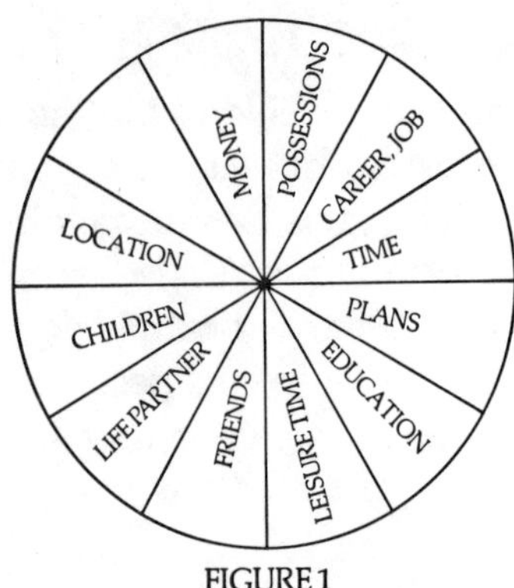


FIGURE 1

Note that the illustration was drawn with a blank space in it. This is for you to fill in with an area that has not been mentioned, one that might be a special battle zone for you in this issue of lordship.

In 1954 I was confronted with a crucial issue. The Lord pointed out to me an area of my life in which I still maintained control. I did not want to submit to the lordship of Christ concerning a life partner. A deep struggle ensued, for I still felt that I should have a part in the choice. God said in effect, "No, you leave it up to me," and the battle lines were drawn.

Finally, after much prayer and seeking counsel, I submitted that area totally to the Lord. I said, "Lord, I am yours. I recognize that everything I have you've given to me. You have my life, and you have this area of my life." Everything changed after that. Men to whom I had been witnessing began to come to Christ. I began to grow. God opened new doors of opportunity. All this came after I finally settled the issue of lordship and made Jesus Christ

Lord of *every* area of my life. For the next six years I concentrated on my ministry with confidence in my heart that God would bring the right person to me at the right time.

Early in 1958 Norma came into my life and I felt led to ask the Lord for his will. For almost two years I prayed about our relationship, seeking guidance from God and promises of his blessing. I also sought the counsel of my spiritual leaders. Early in 1960 I received a most unique promise from Jeremiah 32:39. "I will give them singleness of heart and action, so that they will always fear me for their own good and the good of their children after them." Little did I realize until later that God had given the same promise to Norma. Two months later God spoke to me directly from Romans. "What, then, shall we say in response to this? If God is for us, who can be against us?" (Romans 8:31). When God has been given control, his selection is the very best.

*The Battle of Submission*

When we make the decision to yield to the lordship of Jesus Christ, we immediately find ourself in a battle, a spiritual struggle. We are constantly opposed by Satan and our own will. Many Christians are not willing to enter the battle.

People do not acknowledge Jesus Christ as Lord for many reasons. Four reasons are given here.

*God may ask us to do something we don't want to do.* To many people this is a real barrier to a lordship decision. He may ask us to spend time with someone we would not choose as a friend. He may ask us to move to another part of the country, or to live in a foreign country. When I think of some of the conditions I have seen in some parts of the world that I have visited, I must say, "Yes, Lord, I am willing to go there, but you are going to have to give me the grace to live in that area."

*We think we know what is best for us.* We are looking at life from our point of view rather than God's point of view. Somehow we do not recognize that God always wants the best for us. Yet he who knows the end from the beginning knows what's best for us far better than we do.

*We are not sure that God has our best interests at heart.*[2] This reason is similar to the preceding one, but here it is a matter of not trusting God. We must remember, as Jeremiah recorded, that God has our best interests at heart. "'For I know the plans I have for you,' declares the Lord, 'plans to prosper you and not to harm you, plans to give you hope and a future'" (Jeremiah 29:11).

As you look back on your life, are there some things you might want to change? There probably are many. But would you want to change anything in which you had *clearly* done the will of God? I doubt it. You knew that you were doing what was best for you.

*We're afraid what we give to God may be taken away completely.* This requires surrender, an actual release to God. Here is where we have a real test of faith, for it takes faith to completely surrender anything we cherish to God. It may be a relationship with a person of the opposite sex, a prized possession, an activity, or plans we have made.

I remember a sailor we ministered to in Charleston, South Carolina, who had a real struggle in this area. He had planned to get engaged to his girlfriend, but decided it would be best to get some counsel first. As we discussed the issue, he was challenged to postpone the engagement and completely surrender her to God. During the next few months, having made this commitment, he was repeatedly tested to recommit her to the Lord. Finally, the time came when it was apparent from the growth in both their lives and the ministry he had that God gave her back to him.

Through this experience he gained a new understanding of faith and commitment.

Sometimes God will take away what we give to him. In these cases, we can be sure that it would eventually be wrong for us or possibly destroy our spiritual life and ministry. God graciously cares for those who are his own.

If we're afraid to trust the Lord with our life, then we need to realize that fear and faith are mutually exclusive. He who believes does not fear and he who fears does not really believe. When we trust Jesus Christ as Savior, we turn over our eternal futures completely to him. We do that because we believe that he knows what is best for us.

But what about daily living? Do we believe that he knows what is best for us day by day? The very heart of salvation is that God is thinking of our best interests. If this is so concerning eternity, will it not also be true in daily living? So many of us accept God's offer of salvation by grace through faith, yet insist on staying in the driver's seat for our daily living. How inconsistent can we be? The abundant Christian life depends upon Jesus Christ being our Lord day by day.

*Stages of Obedience*

Obedience is tied into a lordship decision. You cannot separate obedience and submission. Bob Boardman, a missionary in Japan, has identified five stages of obedience. It is good to evaluate our life in light of them periodically.

(1) "I am going to do what I want to do no matter what God wants." Many Christians realize that this is wrong, but they still live according to this pattern. Essentially they do not want Christ to rule their life.

(2) "If God will give me what I want first, then I will give him an equal exchange." This is bargaining with God; I will give him what *I* think is an equal exchange. If God

will only give me the job that I want, then I will give him some of my time in exchange.

(3) "If God will give me what I want first, then I will give him what he wants." This is also bargaining with God. This stage is similar to the second stage, but includes a willingness to give God what he wants.

(4)"I will give God what he wants first, then in faith believe that he will give me what I want." This has finally reversed the "me-first" approach, but it is still a form of bargaining. I am expecting God to do something for me because I have done something for him.

(5) "I will give God whatever he wants, regardless of whether he gives me what I want." This is lordship in practice. This is the crucial stage in our obedience.

* * *

Practicing Christ's lordship is the first essential of becoming a disciple of the Lord Jesus Christ, and it is the most vital one. The remaining nine essentials of discipleship that we will be discussing are built on this one. So I challenge you to evaluate your life and be sure that you are totally submitted to the lordship of Jesus Christ. You can know the fullness of Christian living only when Jesus Christ is Lord. It is the way God has ordained for us to live for him.

---

NOTES: 1. J. Oswald Sanders, *The Pursuit of the Holy* (Grand Rapids, Michigan: Zondervan Publishing House, 1972), p. 65.

2. Walter A. Henrichsen, *Disciples Are Made—Not Born* (Wheaton, Illinois: Victor Books, 1974), pp. 20-23.

CHAPTER

# 4

# PURITY OF LIFE

*A disciple is committed to a life of purity and is taking steps to separate from sin.*

The greatest contrast between unbelievers and believers in this world is in their lifestyle. If the Christian is walking with Jesus Christ as a true disciple, then he is living a life of purity for all to see. If you acknowledge that Jesus is the Lord and Master of your life, then you will live a pure life. In no way can you say that Jesus is your Lord and continue living in sin. A disciple has to know how to conduct himself and live his life in a godly manner. The responsibility for doing so rests squarely on the disciple, but God has promised to help him.

When I first went to Coral Ridge Presbyterian Church, I enrolled in the Evangelism Explosion training program. The first night that we went out calling, I went to Broward General Hospital with Bill Swets, my trainer. He wanted to see a patient there who was interested in our talking to the woman in the bed next to her.

We found the room and Bill began talking to the

woman who was a member of our church. I introduced myself to her roommate. We talked for a while, then I asked her, "What brings you here?"

Without batting an eye, she replied, "A few nights ago I swallowed a whole bottle of sleeping pills. I was trying to end my life."

I quickly shared Jesus Christ with her. When I reached the end of my presentation, I asked her if she would like to receive Christ as her Savior. She really wanted to, so I said, "Let's pray together."

She prayed to receive Jesus—a clear decision for the Lord—and then said, "Well, I guess that means I am going to have to change my style of life now."

She hit the nail right on the head! A Christian disciple's style of life must be different from that of the world around him. It should be drastically different from what it was before he became a Christian.

## Repentance

To repent means to turn around, to make an about-face, to go in the opposite direction. It often results in a drastic change in someone's life. "Just as you used to offer the parts of your body in slavery to impurity and to ever-increasing wickedness, so now offer them in slavery to righteousness leading to holiness" (Romans 6:19). Paul is saying in effect, "Just as you went headlong into sin with complete dedication, never thinking anything about it, now repent and use that same degree of dedication to go toward righteousness and holiness." That is the way God wants Christians to live.

Repentance is not just sorrow. Many people are sorry for their sins, but they do not repent of their sins. Sorrow which is due to a wounded ego is not repentance; sorrow brought on by discovery of a sin is not repentance; neither is sorrow which results from a judgment on sin. A thief may be sorry that he has been caught, but he may not be repentant and will steal again given the opportunity. Among people in the world, sorrow may be remorse over the consequences of the sin. If the sin had never been discovered, there would have been no remorse.

The repentant sinner is sorry that he has offended a holy God and is determined to change. Peter's preaching on the Day of Pentecost included this injunction: "Repent, then, and turn to God, so that your sins may be wiped out, that times of refreshing may come from the Lord" (Acts 3:19). True repentance and conversion always go together. We repent of our sins and turn to God.

Those of us who have repented and been converted are separated unto God to live a holy life. We separate ourself from those influences that would drag us down and prevent our life from being clear reflections of Jesus Christ as Lord and Master. Instead, we consciously pursue holiness. We see an example of the relationship of repentance and conversion to separation and holiness below:

> Flee from sexual immorality. All other sins a man commits are outside his body, but he who sins sexually sins against his own body. Do you not know that your body is a temple of the Holy Spirit, who is in you, whom you have received from God? You are not your own; you were bought at a price. Therefore honor God with your body (1 Corinthians 6:18-20).

Paul also wrote: "'Therefore come out from them and be separate,' says the Lord. 'Touch no unclean thing, and I will receive you'" (2 Corinthians 6:17).

## Evidence of Repentance

A Christian should show evidence of repentance in his or her life. Now the question arises about whose responsibility it is to bring about change in our life. Certainly the Holy Spirit using the Word of God will bring change to our life, but we have to be willing and submissive for him to do so.

During one of our Evangelism Explosion clinics my team called on a young couple and presented the Gospel. Both of them made professions of faith. As I followed them up the next week, I discovered that they were not married but were living together. To make matters worse, the woman was still married to another man from whom she was estranged and by whom she had a baby. I told them that as Christians they could no longer maintain their relationship and that the woman would have to straighten out her marriage situation. They were not responsive.

A week and a half later I received a phone call from the woman at 1:30 in the morning. Even in my sleepiness I recognized her voice and heard her say, "You're right. It is sin. I just slit my wrists!" Down went the phone. I couldn't get to her, but someone else did and saved her life. Here was a woman who recognized that her adulterous relationship was wrong, but she was not willing to change. There was no evidence of repentance. She chose to try suicide rather than trust God to help her in her problems. We must be willing to change with God's help.

When I was overseas I met the sailor who was the yeoman (personal secretary) to the commander of the U.S. Seventh Fleet. The yeoman went everywhere the admiral went. Yet despite his responsible position, on his times off the yeoman committed every sin in the book. Then he met Christ and received him as Savior and Lord. And his life changed completely. It was so drastic a change that word of it spread through the fleet and everyone wanted to know what had happened to him. He was willing to change by the grace of God.

Let us consider four evidences of repentance.

*A Change of Attitudes*

Repentance means a change of attitude, a change of mind. It is an about-face on important issues of life. We must have a change of attitude about God. No longer is he some supreme "Force" out there, but we now know him as Savior and Lord; we realize that he must be Lord of our life in practice.

We must have a change of attitude about sin in our own life. It is no longer something to be played with, but is a transgression against a holy God. We must consciously separate ourself from sin.

We must have a change of attitude about salvation; we must realize that it is God who saved us and not we ourselves—it is by grace through faith (see Ephesians 2:8-9).

We must also change our attitudes about daily issues of life, such as cheating in school or college, what we watch on TV, and our relationships with those closest to us, especially family and friends. All should be affected by our recognition of God's desire for us to live a pure and holy life. What do we do as Christians when the cashier gives us more change than she should? How do we use and spend the money God has given to us? Sensitivity to the Holy Spirit in these areas will help us live a pure life.

*A Change of Desires*

There must also be a change of desires. We no longer desire the ways of the world or material things for ourself, but we become more and more interested in living for God. When a person is outside of Christ, the desires that motivate him are the acquisition of possessions, fame, or a reputation. In our culture we have millions of people—rich and poor alike—who are occupied with materialism. People are concerned with what others think of them. Many are concerned solely with self and the pleasure they can get out of life. Those selfish ambitions should change when a person comes to Christ.

Before salvation we are not interested in the ways of God; we do not care about the Bible. We don't want to go to church or be associated with the people of God. But all that should change and our new desires should be directed toward God and everything concerning him. The Apostle Paul urged, "Set your minds on things above, not on earthly things" (Colossians 3:2). A clear evidence of true repentance is a change of desires.

*An Abhorrence of Sin*

We recognize sin for what it is in the sight of God and we consciously and deliberately turn away from it. A deep sensitivity to sin in our life must come as a result of the Holy Spirit's taking up residence in us. Solomon said this of the righteous person's attitude toward sin: "To fear the Lord is to hate evil; I hate pride and arrogance, evil behavior and perverse speech" (Proverbs 8:13). We avoid evil in every form—in thought, deed, and word. We commit ourself to being governed by the Bible's moral absolutes, including the Ten Commandments. Repentance may be seen in our attitudes toward sin.

*Breaking Off Old Influences*

The last evidence of repentance is that old influences, which often would lead us astray, are broken off. And this is hard to do because it involves people. In some cases, if we continue to associate with the "old crowd," they may drag us down. We may have to make a clean break.

As we grow in our knowledge of Christ, our circle of friends includes more and more Christians. God does not want us to drop all our non-Christian relationships altogether, but he certainly wants us to drop out of the things they do that would draw us back toward sin. We need to minister the gospel to them, but not participate in any sinful activities.

A few years ago a woman came to Christ through our church's Evangelism Explosion program. As I counseled with her in follow-up, she shared with me the sordid circumstances in which she and her husband had been involved in mate-swapping. It was an awful thing as men and women shredded one another for pleasure and the "best match." Now that she had become a Christian she wanted to leave that type of life behind. She made a complete break, worked biblically at destroying the bitterness in her soul and today she is a radiant Christian woman with a tremendous testimony. She and her husband broke off the old influences and began a new way of life.

## God's Standard for Purity of Life

In the Sermon on the Mount Jesus spoke of the kind of life we are to live. "Blessed are the pure in heart, for they will see God" (Matthew 5:8). The promise of seeing God is made to those who are pure in heart. Purity of life begins in our heart. That's why Solomon warned, "Above all else, guard your heart, for it is the wellspring of life" (Proverbs 4:23). One of the seven detestable things to God is "a heart that devises wicked schemes" (Proverbs 6:18).

John, the beloved Apostle, tells us, "For God is greater than our hearts, and he knows everything" (1 John 3:20). God knows all about our propensity to sin, our constant covering it up, our failure to deal the death blow to sinful habits that cripple us.

If God does not reveal any sin in us by his Spirit's gentle touch, we can be assured that we have not offended God, for John writes again, "Dear friends, if our hearts do not condemn us, we have confidence before God" (1 John 3:21). I don't believe God wants us to spend our life in constant morbid introspection. We are sinners and confession restores our fellowship. But we must forgive ourself as well as accept God's forgiveness. All purity begins in the heart of a Christian.

The Apostle Peter also taught about purity.

> Dear friends, I urge you, as aliens and strangers in the world, to abstain from sinful desires, which war against your soul. Live such good lives among the pagans that, though they accuse you of doing wrong, they may see your good deeds and glorify God on the day he visits us (1 Peter 2:11-12).

All impurities of life can be included in that expression "sinful desires." If we are having problems with lustful thoughts or with greed, Peter tells us that we can consciously and deliberately abstain from them. We can drive those thoughts out of our mind. And we do so, of course, through the Word of God.

In the Old Testament David asked, "Who may ascend the hill of the Lord? Who may stand in his holy place?" Then he answered his own question. "He who has clean hands and a pure heart, who does not lift up his soul to an idol or swear by what is false" (Psalm 24:3-4). It is possible for us to stand before God knowing that our heart is pure, if we have confessed our sins to God and received his forgiveness.

We can walk down life's road with our thoughts and actions clean, because God is faithful and has provided the way of victory for us.

## The Battle for Purity

It is not easy to live pure and holy lives in the midst of a sinful and corrupt world. In my training days at Glen Eyrie, Bob Foster, who was then vice-president of The Navigators, used to get the men together at times and speak to us about purity of life. I remember him saying once, "As long as there is red blood flowing through your veins, there is the potential for you to fall. Everyone of us is on common ground in the battle for purity."

Though we live with the potential for falling, there is also the potential for not falling. One of the great statements of the Bible is this: "No temptation has seized you except what is common to man. And God is faithful; he will not let you be tempted beyond what you can bear. But when you are tempted, He will also provide a way out so that you can stand up under it" (1 Corinthians 10:13).

We all experience similar temptations. But God is faithful and provides for all of us the power to say no or to take action that enables us to lead a life of purity. Paul advised Titus:

> For the grace of God that brings salvation has appeared to all men. It teaches us to say "No" to ungodliness and worldly passions, and to live self-controlled, upright, and godly lives in this present age,

> while we wait for the blessed hope—the glorious appearing of our great God and Savior, Jesus Christ, who gave himself for us to redeem us from all wickedness and to purify for himself a people that are his very own, eager to do what is good (Titus 2:11-14).

*The Help of the Holy Spirit*

The Bible clearly tells us that when we receive Jesus Christ as Savior and Lord, the Holy Spirit enters our life and makes our body his temple. The coming of the Holy Spirit to live in us makes us sensitive to sin. Every time we are tempted, the Spirit of God is right there to give us strength to overcome that temptation. We can live victoriously if we trust the enabling grace of God to keep us from practicing sin.

We will still sin, of course, but we will not habitually sin. John says in his first letter, "No one who is born of God will continue to sin, because God's seed remains in him; he cannot go on sinning, because he has been born of God" (1 John 3:9).

Paul cautioned the Ephesians. "And do not grieve the Holy Spirit of God, with whom you were sealed for the day of redemption" (Ephesians 4:30). Who can grieve the Holy Spirit? Only Christians. We grieve him because he lives in us and if we sin, he has to live with that sin in us.

We have the enabling power of the Holy Spirit to live a godly life. But God will not force such a life on us. It is our responsibility to *want* godliness and righteousness and to make the effort to live that way.

We can study the word of God, but unless we do something about what the word of God teaches, we cannot live a pure life. When we do make the effort, the Holy Spirit is the one who works in us enabling us to become pure. We're not doing it alone, but in his almighty power.

A commentator has written:

> The responsibility of the saint is to desire to live a Christlike life, to depend upon the Holy Spirit for the power to live that life, and to step out in faith and live that life. This fulfilled will bring all the infinite resources of grace to the aid of the saint and put in operation all the activities of the Spirit in his behalf.[1]

We will never have victory in this great battle for purity till we allow the Holy Spirit to control our life.

*The Battle Between the Flesh and the Spirit*

As Christians we find ourselves in a constant battle between the flesh, which is our old sinful nature, and the Spirit of God. Paul wrote:

> For the sinful nature desires what is contrary to the Spirit, and the Spirit what is contrary to the sinful nature. They are in conflict with each other, so that you do not do what you want. But if you are led by the Spirit, you are not under law (Galatians 5:17-18).

In this battle for purity, we need to remember that in our flesh there dwells no good thing. Our nature, which we inherited from Adam, has only one propensity and that is to do what is contrary to the law of God. By nature we are all inclined to sin. Our heart and our actions are constantly drawn toward the old nature.

There can be no reconciliation or armistice in this war that is being fought in each of us. The key to victory is in our yielding to God. Paul wrote, "Do not offer the parts of your body to sin, as instruments of wickedness, but rather offer yourselves to God, as those who have been brought from death to life; and offer the parts of your body to him as instruments of righteousness" (Romans 6:13). The choice is ours. Victory depends on the direction in which we yield. If we yield to the old nature, we fall into sin; if we yield to the Spirit, we have victory.

So when we are faced with decisions, when we need counsel, when we are at a crossroads in temptation, when we are inclined to do things our own way, we need to pray over it, and seek the guidance of the Spirit of God in our life to help us make the decision that leads to victory.

*The Example of Paul*

In a significant passage to the church at Rome, the Apostle Paul shares with them—and with us—the battle that was going on in his life (see Romans 7:13-23). His desire was to do right, but he did wrong. This is true with every Christian at one time or another; we want to do what is right in the sight of God, but we end up falling flat on our face.

We find that even though the spirit is willing, the flesh indeed is weak. Paul recognized that in his flesh there dwelt no good thing, and that his tendency was toward breaking the law of God and sinning. He concluded this magnificent passage by telling us: "What a wretched man I am! Who will rescue me from this body of death? Thanks be to God—through Jesus Christ our Lord!" (Romans 7:24-25) The implication is that it is God, and God alone, who will rescue him—and us.

How does God rescue us from this dilemma? What is his answer? Paul continued, "Therefore, there is now no condemnation for those who are in Christ Jesus, because through Christ Jesus the law of the Spirit of life set me free from the law of sin and death" (Romans 8:1-2).

Some years ago when I was learning to fly, I

discovered what this passage meant. There are two laws in flying—the law of gravity, which controls the plane on the ground, and the law of aerodynamics, which causes it to fly. As the forward momentum of the plane increases, the law of aerodynamics sets the plane free from the law of gravity, and the plane leaves the ground. As long as power is available, the plane will fly because of the law of aerodynamics.

If something happens to the power while the plane is in the air, it will slow down, then stall, and eventually crash. The reason for this is that control has passed from the law of aerodynamics to the law of gravity.

This illustrates the two laws Paul was talking about—the law of the Spirit of life and the law of sin and death. As long as we allow the Holy Spirit of God to control our life, to guide and direct us, we operate under the law of the Spirit of life. If we depend on his power, we can have spiritual victory. If we interfere with the source of power, we fall under the law of sin and death.

Many things in this sinful world give us problems. We are constantly tempted to sin. We cannot be victorious over these temptations unless we allow the Holy Spirit to empower us. Paul declared, "For if you live according to the sinful nature, you will die; but if by the Spirit you put to death the misdeeds of the body, you will live, because those who are led by the Spirit of God are sons of God" (Romans 8:13-14).

## Areas of Purity of Life

A number of Old and New Testament passages set forth for us the standards for purity that God expects of his people.

*We Are to Be Pure in Spirit*

The Apostle Paul wrote, "Since we have these promises, dear friends, let us purify ourselves from everything that contaminates body and spirit, perfecting holiness out of reverence for God" (2 Corinthians 7:1). We need to realize that there are sins of impurity in the spirit, in the mind—impure things that we *think* about.

Matthew Henry comments on this passage as follows: "There are sins of the flesh, that are committed with the body, and sins of the spirit, spiritual wickednesses; and we must cleanse ourselves from the filthiness of both, for God is to be glorified both with body and soul."[2] Most sins of impurity originate inside of us, as Jesus so vividly declared (see Mark 7:20-23). So God asks us to be sensitive in our own spirit and depend on his word—his promises—to keep ourself pure in spirit. This attitude of reverence for God will enable us to be holy.

*We Are to Be Pure in Body*

If our mind is under the control of the Holy Spirit, it will make it easier for us to keep our body pure. But we must still work hard at it nevertheless because temptations will surely come, particularly in our sensually oriented culture. Paul spoke to this when he wrote, "It is God's will that you should be holy; that you should avoid sexual immorality; that each of you should learn to control his own body in a way that is holy and honorable, not in passionate lust like the heathen, who do not know God" (1 Thessalonians 4:3-5).

God wants his people to conduct themselves in such a way that their bodies are pure and clean. Notice how sin stains our world and how the results of sin show on the faces and bodies of so many people. We can see this on skid row, in newspaper accounts and pictures, on television, and by personal observation. Sins of impurity exact a heavy toll on human bodies.

*We Are to Be Pure in Our Thoughts*

One of the worst things a Christian can do is to start thinking and daydreaming about impure things. Job is an example of what we must do. He said, "I made a covenant with my eyes not to look lustfully at a girl" (Job 31:1). To the Corinthians, who were surrounded by temptations to impurity, Paul wrote:

> The weapons we fight with are not the weapons of the world. On the contrary, they have divine power to demolish strongholds. We demolish arguments and every pretension that sets itself up against the knowledge of God, and we take captive every thought to make it obedient to Christ (2 Corinthians 10:4-5).

The relationship between a thought and an act is expressed in this poem:

> Sow a thought, reap a word;
> Sow a word, reap an act;
> Sow an act, reap a habit;
> Sow a habit, reap a destiny.

It all begins with a thought. Since our thoughts are subject to sin, they too should be brought under the control of the Holy Spirit. How are you doing in your thought life?

*We Are to Be Pure in Speech*

We are to seek purity in our speech. Questionable jokes or stories should not be part of the Christian's conversation. The Apostle Paul warned, "Do not let any unwholesome talk come out of your mouths, but only what is helpful for building others up according to their needs, that it may benefit those who listen" (Ephesians 4:29). "Nor should there be obscenity, foolish talk or coarse joking, which are out of place, but rather thanksgiving" (Ephesians 5:4).

In other words, we ought to think before we speak; if we would just think, then many of the things we usually say would never pass our lips because we would realize that they are not thoughtful, truthful, and pure.

*We Are to Be Pure in Our Dealings with Others*

The guideline for dealing with others is beautifully expressed by Jesus in the Sermon on the Mount. "In everything, do to others what you would have them do to you, for this sums up the Law and the Prophets" (Matthew 7:12). If we treat people with kindness, honesty, and thoughtfulness, our relationships with them will be good.

Paul challenged the Ephesians with these words:

> Therefore each of you must put off falsehood and speak truthfully to his neighbor, for we are all members of one body. "In your anger do not sin": Do not let the sun go down while you are still angry, and do not give the devil a foothold. He who has been stealing must steal no longer, but must work, doing something useful with his own hands, that he may have something to share with those in need.
>
> Get rid of all bitterness, rage and anger, brawling and slander, along with every form of malice. Be kind and compassionate to one another, forgiving each other, just as in Christ God forgave you (Ephesians 4:25-28, 31-32).

We need to be sensitive to the Spirit of God and to his leading in the way we handle ourself with people, and follow the teaching of Jesus when he said, "Let your light shine before men, that they may see your good deeds and praise your Father in heaven" (Matthew 5:16).

*We Are to Be Pure in Our Business Dealings*

This involves honesty. In our materialistic society men and women in business often do things in dishonest ways. It is easy for Christians who are not alert to get trapped into conducting business in the same dishonest way. The business world has sometimes been the place where a man who had a good testimony in his church has lost it because of failure to conduct himself in his business with honesty and purity.

In the New Testament we are urged to be industrious and honest toward men, business, and government.

*We Are to Be Pure in Personal Relationships*

Purity is absolutely vital in a marital relationship. Each of us who is married must constantly ask ourself the question, Am I faithful to my marriage vows?

Many believe that infidelity and dishonesty in the marital relationship are the causes of the rampaging divorce rate in America today. In ever increasing numbers, Christians are becoming part of those tragic statistics. Quite often it is due to the fact that men and women have not made a solemn vow to God that they would remain faithful to their spouse. Purity in the marriage relationship is an absolute must for the Christian.

Our relationships with our friends must also be based on purity. We need each other, for as the Bible says, "As iron sharpens iron, so one man sharpens another" (Proverbs 27:17). Solomon also said, "A man of many companions may come to ruin, but there is a friend who sticks closer than a brother" (Proverbs 18:24). One honest, caring friend is more valuable than many casual acquaintances. Real friendships result from sharing our life with other people.

Part of our responsibility as a friend is accepting and giving rebuke. It is by this means that we are able to help one another withstand temptation and remain pure.

* * *

The battle for purity is a matter of choice, a matter of obedience to God, a matter of commitment to him to live his way. But when we do fall, we need to recognize that we have sinned, then confess it immediately and seek God's forgiveness. We can then know that the sin is forgiven, our life is cleansed, and that God accepts us on the basis of the finished work of Jesus Christ on the cross of Calvary.

---

NOTES: 1. Kenneth S. Wuest, *Galatians in the Greek New Testament: For the English Reader*, 3rd edition (Grand Rapids, Michigan: Wm. B. Eerdmans Publishing Company, 1944), p. 162

2. Matthew Henry, *Matthew Henry's Commentary On the Whole Bible*, 6 vols. (Old Tappan, New Jersey: Fleming H. Revell Company, n.d.), 6:n.p.

# CHAPTER 5
# DEVOTIONS AND PRAYER

*A disciple has a daily devotional time and is developing in his prayer life.*

As we received Christ by faith, so we should live by faith daily. And that comes only as we are in the word of God. "Consequently, faith comes from hearing the message, and the message is heard through the word of Christ" (Romans 10:17). You will discover as you spend time with God alone, reading and meditating on his word and praying, that he ministers to you through his Holy Spirit and your faith grows on a daily basis. Anyone who has a living, vibrant relationship with God will testify that it is due to the quality of the time he spends in God's word and prayer.

## Examples of the Quiet Time

What authority do we as Christians have for spending time alone with God on a daily basis? We ask this because nowhere in the Bible is there a commandment which says, "Thou shalt have a daily quiet time!" No precepts or directives are given, but some very strong examples are: Jesus met with his heavenly Father regularly throughout his busy ministry; the Psalms record for us many instances of a man spending time alone in the presence of God; the biographies of great Christian men and women emphasize their habit of spending time alone with God.

*The Example of Jesus*

The practice of Jesus should be sufficient to show us the importance of our daily devotions. Early in his ministry we find him setting time aside to meet with the Father. Mark records for us, "Very early in the morning, while it was still dark, Jesus got up, left the house and went off to a solitary place, where he prayed" (Mark 1:35). The significance of this is obvious when you consider the circumstances of the previous day. Jesus spent time in the synagogue in Capernaum teaching. While there he healed a man who was possessed by an evil spirit. After he left the synagogue, Jesus went to the home of Simon and Andrew. There he healed Simon's mother-in-law. After sunset many people gathered at the home to be healed of various diseases.

What kind of day did Jesus have? He was extremely busy. Most of us after a day like that would want to stay in bed the next morning. Throughout Jesus' ministry most days were just like that, but he took the time to rise early in the morning to pray. He had been busy until well after sunset, but he was up before sunrise.

*Examples in the Psalms*

The Psalms are full of expressions of devotion to the Lord. This means that the men who wrote these marvelous psalms had a vital relationship with him. David wrote: "Let the morning bring me word of your unfailing love, for I have put my trust in you. Show me the way I should go, for to you I lift up my soul" (Psalm 143:8). He also wrote: "Blessed is the man you choose and bring near to live in your courts! We are filled with the good things of your house, of your holy temple" (Psalm 65:4). In my Bible I have written the words *quiet time* by this verse.

David pours out his heart about his need for fellowship with God in this psalm:

O God, you are my God,
  earnestly I seek you;
my soul thirsts for you,
  my body longs for you,
in a dry and weary land
  where there is no water.
I have seen you in the sanctuary
  and beheld your power and your glory.
Becau your love is better than life,
  my lips will glorify you.
I will praise you as long as I live,
  and in your name I will lift up my hands.
My soul will be satisfied as with the richest of
  foods;
  with singing lips my mouth will praise you.
On my bed I remember you;
  I think of you through the watches of the night.
Because you are my help,
  I sing in the shadow of your wings.
I stay close to you;
  your right hand upholds me (Psalm 63:1-8).

Another psalmist wrote, "It is good to praise the Lord

and make music to your name, O Most High, to proclaim your love in the morning and your faithfulness at night" (Psalm 92:1-2). As you study this passage and others like it, the following pattern emerges; thanking God for his love in the morning and his faithfulness at night. Lorne Sanny, president of The Navigators, has made this evening prayer a habit in his life. He once shared how he prays through the day backwards before going to bed, to thank the Lord for his faithfulness to him.

*Examples of Men and Women of God*

The missionary biography that made the greatest impact on my life is the story of J. O. Fraser recorded in *Behind the Ranges.*[1] Fraser worked among the Lisu tribe in southwestern China in the early 20th century. The principles of evangelism, making disciples, and particularly the maintenance of the personal life before God are outstanding in this biography. Fraser tells of the struggles he went through and emphasizes that everything he did effectively emerged out of his time alone with God.

Dawson Trotman, founder and first president of The Navigators, was a man who strongly emphasized the quiet time as a necessary spiritual exercise. His biographer records a series of events that paved the way for the subsequent ministry of The Navigators.[2] Daws and a friend covenanted with God to meet in the hills near Los Angeles each morning at 4 o'clock to pray for the needs of their ministry. They began praying for Long Beach, California, then moved to praying for San Pedro and Los Angeles, then for other cities in the state. When God expanded their vision, they brought a map up to their hillside sanctuary, put their fingers on different states and prayed, "Lord, give us a ministry in Alabama . . . Connecticut . . . Illinois . . ." and so on through the states. As God expanded their vision further, they brought a world map up there and began praying for countries such as New Zealand, Canada, Argentina, and China. They met for forty-two consecutive days before God lifted the burden, but it set a pattern for Trotman's life. He met daily with the Lord early in the morning the rest of his days.

Dawson Trotman saw the answers to these prayers begin coming in his lifetime. During World War II men from every state came to the Savior and were built up in the faith. They made an impact in the military services and in the many countries in which they served. Roy Robertson was the first Navigator missionary and went to China in 1948. The work grew in Asia and developed in Australia, New Zealand, and Europe. George Sanchez became the first Navigator representative in Latin America. The week Trotman died, five Navigator men arrived in Nairobi, Kenya to begin the work in Africa. Navigator trained men and women have touched lives on all the continents of the world.

One of the means of ministry God has enabled The Navigators to develop for community outreach is *The 2:7 Series*, a discipleship training program for church laymen.[3] (The series of six courses is named after Colossians 2:7, in which Paul says that we are to be "rooted and built up in him, strengthened in the faith as you were taught, and overflowing with thankfulness.") One of the features of this study course is the *Bible Reading Highlights Record*, on which the participants record what God emphasized in their quiet time. It has been a real thrill for me to hear people in my 2:7 groups share what they have been getting out of a daily time alone with God. I often see them flipping through their pages, and I see that all of them are filled in. Exciting things happen in a person's life when they commit themself to a regular time alone with God each day.

## Fellowship with God

The purpose of a quiet time is not to serve as a magical energizer that will keep us going throughout the day. It is a time when we have fellowship with Almighty God. The Bible teaches us that God desires this time with us and that the basis of the fellowship is the death on the cross of Jesus Christ.

### *Christ Made Fellowship Possible*

In Old Testament times in Israel, God ordained that sacrifices be offered morning and evening, a symbolic preview of what Jesus would accomplish on the cross. It was at the mercy seat that God met with his people Israel. But now every one of us can meet with God each day. The death of Jesus Christ on the cross of Calvary has provided the basis for our daily fellowship with the living God. Because of the salvation that Jesus achieved on that cross, and the reconciliation I now enjoy, it is possible to have communion and fellowship with the holy and righteous God.

The writer to the Hebrews declared:

> Therefore, brothers, since we have confidence to enter the Most Holy Place by the blood of Jesus, by a new and living way opened for us through the curtain, that is, his body, and since we have a great priest over the house of God, let us draw near to God with a sincere heart in full assurance of faith, having our hearts sprinkled to cleanse us from a guilty conscience and having our bodies washed with pure water (Hebrews 10:19-22).

We have direct access to God through the merit of Jesus Christ's death on Calvary.

### *God Desires Fellowship with Us*

The amazing thing we find in Scripture is that God wants to have fellowship with us. What a staggering thought it is to realize that the Almighty God, creator of heaven and earth, wants to commune with *me* and is waiting for me to spend time with him. Jesus told the Samaritan woman at Jacob's well, "Yet a time is coming and has now come when the true worshipers will worship the Father in spirit and truth, for they are the kind of worshipers the Father seeks" (John 4:23).

The living God seeks our fellowship; he wants us to fellowship with him! We need to remember that God is waiting for us to meet with him in the morning or evening or whenever it works best for us. Everything else aside, this should motivate us for our quiet times with him.

## THE PLACE OF THE BIBLE

One of the means of communication with God in our quiet time is the Bible. Let's look at some practical ways we can use the Bible.

### *Spiritual Nourishment*

In our quiet time we need to have an objective as we get together with God. Our quiet time should not be lesson preparation for Sunday school or a Bible study. God may give us something in our quiet time that we can use in a ministry, but it should not be our objective to seek something specifically for that. We cannot really minister to others if we have neglected our own spiritual nourishment.

The objective we should have in our devotional time is to be fed spiritually, to be nourished by God's word. We should become more intimately acquainted with Jesus Christ, get to know more about what he has done for us, and discover what is on his heart and mind. All that can only come through the word of God.

*Follow a Plan*

Many people who try to have a quiet time without a definite plan in mind soon stop meeting with God. You must choose or develop a plan by which you are going to get something for your life from God and give to him the fellowship he desires.

One plan would be to use something like the *Devotional Diary*,[4] which arranges Bible readings for you and provides a Quiet Time Work Sheet for each day of the year on which to record the thoughts God gives you during your devotional time.

Another plan is the one recommended by Jim Downing and discussed at length in his book *Meditation: The Bible Tells You How*.[5] Briefly, what he suggests is reading the psalm that corresponds to the day's date and every thirtieth psalm after it. For example, if today is the 12th, you would read Psalms 12, 42, 72, 102, and 132. In addition you would read one proverb. Using the same example, that would be Proverbs 12.

A third possibility would be to pick a book of the Bible. Ask God to speak through the verses to you and make a commitment to do what you are told. The greatest profit we can have from our quiet time with God is to apply God's word to our life. Ask yourself these questions about the passage you are reading:

- Is there an example for me to follow?
- Is there a command for me to obey?
- Is there any error for me to avoid?
- Is there any sin for me to renounce?

- Is there any promise for me to claim?
- Is there any new thought about God himself?
- Is there any new thought about Jesus Christ?
- Is there any new thought about the Holy Spirit's ministry in my life?

This simple plan will help you meditate on God's word and get some spiritual sustenance from the passage. Personally, I have found great help in asking these simple questions, and have often discovered a specific truth that God wanted to give me that day for personal meditation and application.

## THE PLACE OF PRAYER

The other means of communication with God during a quiet time is prayer. God speaks to us through his word, then we converse with him through prayer.

### *The Cost of Prayer*

God has made himself accessible to us, yet so few believers avail themselves of the opportunity to talk with God. One of the reasons for this is that prayer is costly, and people who are not disciples are not willing to pay the price.

It takes time and effort to converse with God through prayer. Christian biographies of godly men and women throughout history reveal that those who did anything worthwhile for God were people of prayer, spending much time on their knees before him. And that is costly.

Everything in our world wars against prayer. Men who do not believe in God will not allow time off for prayer. The devil does not want the people of God to pray. Our busy lives interfere with times of prayer. We all have to fight the "tyranny of the urgent."[6] Rising early in the morning to pray is very difficult for many of us. Our body resists it; our minds resists it; and Satan resists it. But we must pray. It is our necessary lifeline to God.

Missionaries have said that prayer is the hardest thing they have to do. It is far easier to do evangelism than pray. Language study is easier than prayer. Learning about a foreign culture is easier than praying.

When I went overseas to minister to American servicemen in Japan, I found that the hardest thing I had to do was maintain my daily relationship with God and pray consistently. Why? Because of the extent of the ministry. There was so much to do that there seemed to be little time left for praying. If you as a Christian disciple commit yourself to the quiet time and to prayer, you will find there is a daily cost.

*Follow a Plan*

We can come to God in prayer through the use of one of the following plans.

*C-P-T-I-P.* The first plan utilizes five words as follows:

C—Confession
P—Praise
T—Thanksgiving
I—Intercession
P—Petition

*C—Confession.* The first step in praying is confession of all known sin to be sure the channel of communication is open. As we do this, we join David in asking God to look into our heart. "Search me, O God, and know my heart; test me and know my anxious thoughts. See if there is any offensive way in me, and lead me in the way everlasting" (Psalm 139:23-24). As God searches our heart and places his finger on things that are displeasing to him, we confess our sins and ask him for forgiveness (see 1 John 1:9).

The psalmist recognized the need for this and said, "If I had cherished sin in my heart, the Lord would not have listened; but God has surely listened and heard my voice in prayer" (Psalm 66:18-19). Solomon declared, "He who conceals his sins does not prosper, but whoever confesses and renounces them finds mercy" (Proverbs 28:13).

*P—Praise*. After we have been cleansed, it is a good thing to continue our time of prayer with praise to God. Praise expresses our adoration and our love for him. As we praise God, our thoughts should be focused on who he is, his greatness, power, majesty, love, grace, mercy, and longsuffering.

You may want to use passages from his word that you have memorized. Many have found this to be extremely helpful in times of prayer. One of the most beautiful prayers of praise is that of David toward the end of his life (see 1 Chronicles 29:10-13).

*T—Thanksgiving*. We need to learn to be a thankful people. Every day of our life we have something for which we can thank our Lord. We can thank him for our health, for his provision for all our needs, for safety, for the joyful times in our life, for friends, our church, and for the privilege of walking with Jesus Christ. You may want to sit down and make a list of all the things you ought to thank him for and then pray through the list. Remember to thank him for trials and difficult times as well, for they are intended for our benefit.

It is interesting to note that in the description of unsaved and rebellious people, Paul includes thanklessness. "For although they knew God, they neither glorified him as God nor gave thanks to him, but their thinking became futile and their foolish hearts were darkened" (Romans 1:21).

*I—Intercession.* We are responsible to pray for others. Many of us glibly promise to pray for people, but then we forget and do not intercede for them. One of the most helpful things we can do is to keep a prayer list on which we write down their names and requests. Then in our prayer time we can go over the list and pray for them specifically.

We should pray regularly for our pastors, Sunday school teachers, and missionaries. We should pray for those with whom we work, as well as for our family and friends who are close to us.

We pray for others in the same way that we pray for ourselves, for our needs as human beings and as Christians are essentially the same. We can trust God to meet the needs of others as he does our own.

*P—Petition.* Finally, we need to pray for ourself and our personal needs. Whatever these may be, we can bring them to God and expect him to answer. We should pray for specific things for which we expect specific answers. A great encouragement to me has been to look over old prayer lists and see how God, in his own marvelous grace and provision, has answered my prayers. As we pray in his will, according to his word, we have the assurance of Scripture that he will hear and answer.

*A-C-T-S.* Another plan for prayer is based on four words:

A—Adoration
C—Confession
T—Thanksgiving
S—Supplication

The order and words used vary, but the elements are basically the same as C—P—T—I—P.

## ATTITUDE

*Let Your Heart Be Still*

The gems of God are not ours to examine by rushing into his presence. We need to approach God in quietness. The psalmist recorded, "Be still, and know that I am God" (Psalm 46:10). Through Isaiah God said, "In quietness and trust is your strength" (Isaiah 30:15). When our heart is still before him, he is able to speak to us through his word and give us that which we need for the day. If we are in a hurry, we may miss something of value.

*Expect His Presence*

We must expect God to minister to us. If we expose our life to God and invite him into the innermost recesses of our heart, we will know his presence with us. So be quiet, concentrate on his word, and expect the presence of God through his spirit. Anytime we expectantly read God's word, he will speak to us.

We can certainly read our Bible and say our prayers to our own satisfaction, but we lose the value of communion with the living God if we do not develop the closeness and fellowship that we can have with him. We need to be aware of the danger of our quiet times becoming just something we do because of force of habit. Each meeting with God should be a time of anticipation because of our knoweldge that he wants this fellowship with us and is waiting for us to come into his presence.

If we are not getting anything out of our quiet times, we need to see if there is some sin in our life that has not been confessed and that is hindering God from ministering to us. Or perhaps we are only reading God's word with our mind and not meditating on it with our heart. An excellent booklet to read in this area is *A Primer on Meditation.*[7]

## TIME AND PLACE

It's very easy for us to make excuses for not spending time alone with God. We may be convinced that they can't be overcome. Many people blame the lack of time and/or place. The key is that we must be committed to the fact that this is totally necessary for our spiritual life and then maintain that discipline day after day.

Bob Foster writes about the quiet time in one of his *Challenge* letters.

> It was in 1882 on the campus of Cambridge University that the world was first given the slogan: "Remember the morning watch."
>
> Students like Hooper and Thornton found their days "loaded" with studies, games, lectures, and bull sessions. Enthusiasm and activity were the order of the day. These dedicated men soon discovered a flaw in their spiritual armor—a small crack which if not soon closed, would bring disaster.
>
> They sought an answer and came up with a scheme they called the morning watch—the plan to spend the first minutes of a new day alone with God, praying and reading the Bible.
>
> The morning watch sealed the crack. It enshrined a truth so often obscured by the pressure of ceaseless activity that it needs daily rediscovery: To know God, it is necessary to spend consistent time with him.
>
> The idea caught fire. "A remarkable period of religious blessing" followed, and culminated in the departure of the Cambridge Seven, a band of prominent athletes and men of wealth and education for missionary service. They gave up everything to go out to China for Christ.[8]

Each one of us is responsible to determine what time is best for us. Since most of us in our society have fixed times for our meals, why not a fixed time for something more important—our spiritual meals with God? The best way to guarantee that you will have your quiet time is to set aside a fixed time for that purpose.

Many have chosen to set aside time in the morning. For some people it may be late in the evening when things have calmed down in their day. For others it might be a quiet time in the middle of the day when they can be alone.

Decide what time best suits your schedule, and then stick to it. Make it a lordship commitment to God.

At Glen Eyrie, The Navigators' headquarters in Colorado, we have a beautiful sixty-six-room Tudor castle. Today it is used for conference housing the year round, but many years ago when I worked there, it was used as men's housing during the winter months. A number of us lived in each of the large rooms and shared a bathroom. Some of the men had desks in the rooms, some in other parts of the castle, but there were not enough quiet places to go around. Furthermore, most of us got up around the same time. Yet in the midst of the busyness of that time, men could successfully have their devotions in the same room where others were still getting ready. They had learned how to have a quiet time by mentally shutting out the world.

* * *

God wants us to have time with him. He invites us into his presence. He speaks to us through his word and we speak back to him through prayer. We must commit ourself daily to this vital meeting with him.

C.T. Studd, English missionary statesman at the turn

of the century, throughout his Christian life got up at 4:30 in the morning to meet with the Lord. Of the importance of that time he said, "If you don't desire to meet the Devil during the day, meet Jesus before dawn."[9]

---

NOTES:

1. Mrs. Howard Taylor, *Behind the Ranges* (London: The Lutterworth Press, 1956).
2. Betty Lee Skinner, *Daws* (Grand Rapids, Michigan: Zondervan Publishing House, 1974), p. 62.
3. *The 2:7 Series* is available only through attending a training program and becoming qualified to lead it, or by joining a group to go through the series. You may obtain information about how to join one in your area or be trained to lead one by writing to The 2:7 Coordinator, The Navigators, P.O. Box 20, Colorado Springs, Colorado 80901.
4. The *Devotional Diary*, published by NavPress, is obtainable from your local Christian bookstore.
5. Jim Downing, *Meditation: The Bible Tells You How* (Colorado Springs, Colorado: NavPress, 1976), pp. 41-45.
6. This term comes from a booklet by that name, *Tryanny of the Urgent*, by Charles E. Hummel (Downers Grove, Illinois: InterVarsity Press, 1967).
7. Robert D. Foster, *A Primer on Meditation* (Colorado Springs, Colorado: NavPress, n.d.).
8. Robert D. Foster, *Seven Minutes with God.* (NavPress).
9. Norman P. Grubb, *C.T. Studd* (Chicago: Moody Press, 1962), p. 168.

# CHAPTER 6
# THE IMPORTANCE OF THE BIBLE

*A disciple demonstrates faithfulness and a desire to learn and apply the word of God through hearing it preached and taught, reading it frequently, Bible study, Scripture memory, and meditation on the Scriptures.*

In this chapter we want to discuss two major areas—why God gave us the Bible and how we go about being in his word. If we know the reasons why we have been given something, it improves our effectiveness in making use of it.

## Why God Gave Us the Bible

The Bible is the means by which God has revealed himself to mankind. In it are all the things we need to know for faith and practice. It is God's final word to man about living in this world and knowing we have eternal life.

### *The Bible Reveals the God of Salvation to Us*

James tells us that God "chose to give us birth through the word of truth, that we might be a kind of firstfruits of all he created" (James 1:18). Peter wrote, "For you have been born again, not of perishable seed, but of imperishable, through the living and enduring word of God" (1 Peter 1:23). It is through the word of God that we recognize and acknowledge our need of a Savior from sin. The Holy Spirit uses the Scriptures to reveal the needs of people. The new birth comes through this word of truth. That's why the heart of evangelism is the communication of the plan of salvation from the Bible.

The Bible explicitly tells us that everything that has been written in it was "to teach us, so that through endurance and the encouragement of the Scriptures we might have hope" (Romans 15:4). The biblical concept of hope has in it the sense of certainty, of knowing that we have eternal life with God.

The psalmist wrote, "Salvation is far from the wicked, for they do not seek out your decrees" (Psalm 119:155). What the psalmist is saying is that no one will be saved apart from the word of God. The wicked do not find salvation because they will not consider the Scriptures, which are used by the Holy Spirit to pierce our heart and bring us to God through Jesus Christ.

*The Bible Cleanses Us from Our Sins*

The disciple is responsible to lead a pure life. In order to lead a pure life, the disciple must be sensitive to sin. The only way we can be sensitive to sin is to be in the word of God, which enables us to recognize our sins. We confess them to God, and so are cleansed from them. No one can ever sit down with his Bible, read it carefully, and not experience the ministry of the Holy Spirit dealing with him about certain sins in his life. One of the reasons so many Christians are slothful and unfruitful is because of the lack of this ministry of God's word in their lives.

The psalmist once asked, "How can a young man keep his way pure?" And he quickly answered: "By living according to your word. I seek you with all my heart; do not let me stray from your commands. I have hidden your word in my heart that I might not sin against you" (Psalm 119:9-11). Note that it says "might not sin against you," not "cannot." We can still sin if we choose to. We have to allow God's word to be a cleansing agent by obeying it.

I experienced a time as a Christian when I was not growing. I had some problems in my life, some habits that I knew were not right, but I couldn't do anything about them. I was not feeding on the word of God because I did not know the Bible was food for my soul. Then a sailor introduced me to the Bible and to Scripture memory and I began to feed my soul with the word of God. I confessed sins as they were revealed to me and was cleansed. In a while I began to notice that some of those habits that had gripped my life were beginning to leave me. The word of God had a cleansing effect on my life and washed those habits right out of it.

If you are having problems with undesirable habits, the answer is to get into the word of God. Regular Bible study, Scripture memory, and application of God's word to your life will do wonders for you. A regular diet of the word of God enables the Holy Spirit to use the Scriptures to deal with our sins.

### *The Bible Enables Us to Grow Spiritually*

The Christian disciple must grow spiritually. If he doesn't, he is stagnating and is not really a disciple. Our spiritual growth is directly dependent on our consistent intake of the word of God as our spiritual food.

The writer to the Hebrews divides biblical intake into milk and meat. "In fact, though by this time you ought to be teachers, you need someone to teach you the elementary truths of God's word all over again. You need milk, not solid food!" (Hebrews 5:12). New converts need the milk of the word so that they can begin to grow through that intake of spiritual nourishment (see 1 Peter 2:2-3).

The disciple, however, ought to be taking in "solid food" or "meat" for growth beyond the "newborn" stage. Milk will help us grow to a certain point (just like physical children), but after that we will need meat for continued spiritual growth. We are built up and progress in our sanctification by the word of God. It is an important principle in our spiritual growth, for we have the capacity to continue growing spiritually throughout our Christian life.

When Paul addressed the elders of the church at Ephesus, he was speaking to a group of men who were certainly disciples. He challenged them with these words: "Now I commit you to God and to the word of his grace, which can build you up and give you an inheritance among all those who are sanctified" (Acts 20:32).

### *The Bible Guides and Directs Us through Life*

The disciple looks to the word of God for guidance concerning the will of God for his life. God has promised to lead us, but in order to know what God has for us, we must be in his word. Solomon encourages us to "trust in the Lord with all your heart and lean not on your own understanding; in all your ways acknowledge him, and he will make your paths straight" (Proverbs 3:5-6).

If we trust God concerning the direction of our life, he promises to give us some of our innermost desires that are according to his will. The psalmist wrote: "Delight yourself in the Lord and he will give you the desires of your heart. Commit your way to the Lord; trust in him and he will do this" (Psalm 37:4-5).

One of my friends had a great desire to visit a certain city in the Middle East. He had claimed the promise in Psalm 37:4-5 and had prayed about it for some time. He had confidence that God would honor this desire in his own timing. On one occasion as he was about to start on an around-the-world trip in his ministry with The Navigators, a friend of his came up to him and said, "Say, I've got some extra money and the Lord has laid it on my heart to give it to you to use for something that you've been praying about for a long time." The friend had not known about his desire to visit this city, but God in his timing and through his obedient servant provided for my friend.

If we are delighting ourself in the Lord by being in the word of God and a holy desire comes to us, then God will fulfill it in his time and in his way.

*The Bible Empowers Us in Our Evangelism*

Another reason the disciple is to be in the word of God is so that he might witness effectively for Christ. We can never be effective in leading people to the Savior unless we know the Scriptures. We have to have something to say to unbelievers. God told Ezekiel: "The people to whom I am sending you are obstinate and stubborn. Say to them, 'This is what the Sovereign Lord says'" (Ezekiel 2:4).

That's what God specifically commissioned Paul to do. "Then he (Ananias) said: 'The God of our fathers has chosen you to know his will and to see the Righteous One and to hear words from his mouth. You will be his witness to all men of what you have seen and heard'" (Acts 22:14-15). So Paul wrote:

> God was reconciling the world to himself in Christ, not counting men's sins against them. And he has com-

> mitted to us the message of reconciliation. We are therefore Christ's ambassadors, as though God were making his appeal through us. We implore you on Christ's behalf: Be reconciled to God (2 Corinthians 5:19-20).

Our message when we witness should be, "This is what God says!" An ambassador does not say what he wants to say, but only what he is told to say.

A striking passage on the necessity of the word of God for a strong witness is found in Solomon's Proverbs. God speaking through the writer said, "Have I not written thirty [excellent] sayings for you, sayings of counsel and knowledge, teaching you true and reliable words, so that you can give sound answers to him who sent you?" (Proverbs 22:20-21).

As a young Christian I knew that the men around me in the Navy needed the Savior. I tried to witness about Christ, but I did not know the Scriptures. I only got into arguments with the men. Then I got into the word of God, began to memorize Scripture, and learned a simple gospel presentation. Three months after I started feeding on God's word,I led a sailor to Christ.

God has given us the Bible so that we might be effective witnesses for him.

*The Bible Helps Us Live the Life of a Disciple*

In a most significant passage of Scripture, which in effect summarizes the previous reasons why the Scriptures were given, Paul stated, "All Scripture is God-breathed and is useful for teaching, rebuking, correcting and training in righteousness, so that the man of God may be thoroughly equipped for every good work" (2 Timothy 3:16-17).

*A disciple needs teaching.* Teaching or doctrine is the basis of everyone's living. People may have false concepts or wrong premises, but they are basing their lives on some teaching. You can tell quite a bit about a man's or a woman's doctrine by the manner of that person's life.

For Christian disciples, teaching must come from the word of God. Everything in our Christian life—our character, our words, our actions, our experiences—is related to biblical teaching or "doctrine". The Scripture is what we believe in and what we do; it is the basis of our faith, its very foundation.

When we arrived in San Antonio on one of our ministry assignments, we began attending a church that was strong in Bible exposition. The first Sunday we were there, the pastor taught from Romans 3:21. On our first anniversary in that church, he was teaching Romans 5:21. In one year of preaching through Romans verse by verse on Sunday mornings, Sunday nights, and Wednesday nights, he had only gone through two chapters. At this pace you could understand the Bible, assimilate it, and apply it practically to your life. It was a rewarding and uplifting time for us that year.

*A disciple needs rebuking.* In order for us to live our Christian life as a disciple, we need the Scriptures to rebuke us, to reveal to us how we have sinned, and where we have missed the mark. The Holy Spirit will faithfully show us these areas as we are in the Scriptures. It is one of the responsibilities of the Spirit to take the word of God and rebuke us concerning the sins that we commit. The Bible serves as a mirror to show us exactly what we are like. Some people do not want to be in the Bible because it will reveal their sins to them.

*A disciple needs correcting.* The Bible not only tells us we have sinned, but it also provides the corrective steps necessary for the restoration of fellowhship with God and with our fellowmen. In other words, the Bible tells us how we can get back to where we ought to be in the life of discipleship. We are not left dangling in our sins, but God graciously points out to us what we need to do to get on the right track.

*A disciple needs training in righteousness.* The Bible tells us how to live a life pleasing to God, how to live harmoniously with our fellowmen, both Christians and non-Christians, and how to live in this world under the domination of the evil one. Our responsibility is on two planes—vertically to God and horizontally to men.

The horizontal path in Figure 2 is the life of discipleship that we should be living. But for all of us there are times when we sin and go off on a tangent. We get off the "straight and narrow" path. At first we may not notice it because we are still so close to the right track, but after a while it deviates further. Most sins do not show themselves as a sudden, abrupt change, and so sometimes are hard to recognize. But after a certain time, when we have strayed some distance from the right path, the Holy Spirit rebukes us through God's word and we are faced with a choice. We can disregard him and keep going farther and farther away from God's ways. Or we can take steps of corrective action and return to the word of God for further training in righteousness.

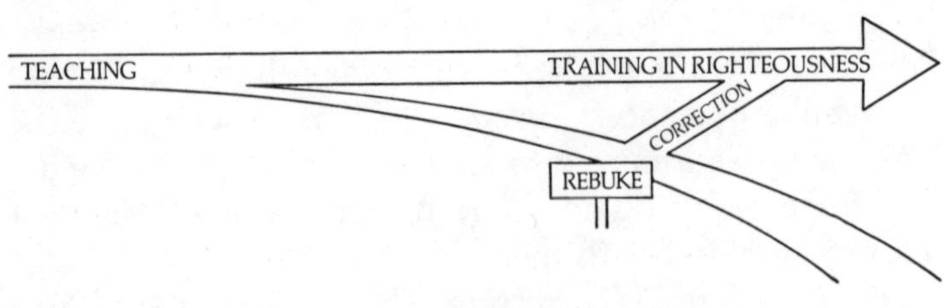


FIGURE 2

## How We Get to Know the Bible

God's word teaches us that we can get into the Scriptures in a number of ways. We hear the word of God, we read it, we study it, we memorize it, and we meditate on what we have heard, read, studied, and memorized. In The Navigators we have used the Hand Illustration (see Figure 3) as a way of emphasizing the five means of intake of the word of God.

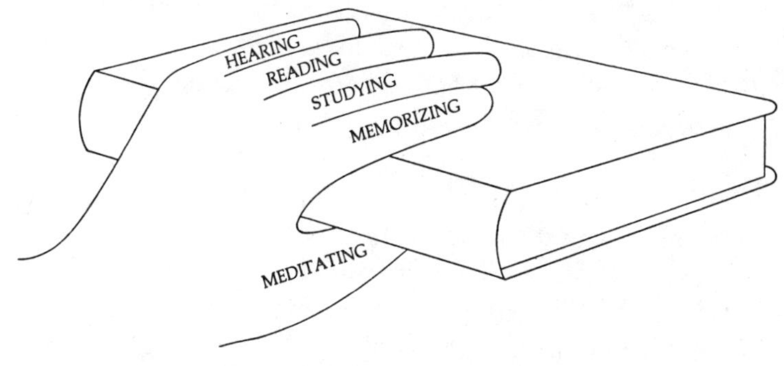


FIGURE 3

### *Hearing the Word of God*

Our first responsibility is to hear the word of God regularly from godly teachers. Morning and evening worship are excellent means of this intake. When you hear the word preached, a servant of God is communicating the Lord's message to you. We can also hear the word of God in Sunday school or a training class. We can hear it on the radio and television. We can hear it at conferences, seminars, and on tapes. Paul wrote, "Consequently, faith comes from hearing the message, and the message is heard through the word of Christ" (Romans 10:17).

To help you remember what you have heard, make it a practice to take notes. You see, a disciple is not merely a hearer of the word of God, but he is a doer of it.

> Do not merely listen to the word, and so deceive yourselves. Do what it says. Anyone who listens to the word but does not do what it says is like a man who looks at his face in a mirror and, after looking at himself, goes away and immediately forgets what he looks like. But the man who looks intently into the perfect law that gives freedom, and continues to do this, not forgetting what he has heard, but doing it—he will be blessed in what he does (James 1:22-25).

In order to apply the Scriptures, one has to make specific plans for doing it. That requires notetaking.

A young woman in my class at Coral Ridge Presbyterian Chuch shared with me that when she first came to the church, Dr. Kennedy's preaching "hooked" her. She heard things she had never heard before and became interested. Her faith grew as she listened to the word of the Lord.

*Reading the Word of God*

As discussed in Chapter 4, we should also be reading the word of God regularly. We should have a plan that will enable us to read through the whole Bible once a year or at least once every two years.

In ancient Israel the king was required to read the word of God "all the days of his life so that he may learn to revere the Lord his God and follow carefully all the words of this law and these decrees" (Deuteronomy 17:19). John promised blessings for those who would read God's word (see Revelation 1:3), and Paul urged Timothy to devote himself to the public reading of the Scriptures (see 1 Timothy 4:13). Christian disciples should be reading the word of God regularly.

*Studying the Word of God*

The third vital means of intake of the word of God is study or careful investigation of the Scriptures. King Solomon urged us to search for wisdom as though we were looking for silver and treasure (see Proverbs 2:4). The Bible is the source of all wisdom. Paul told Timothy to "do your best to present yourself to God as one approved, a workman who does not need to be ashamed and who correctly handles the word of truth" (2 Timothy 2:15). The Bible commends the "noble" Bereans because they "examined the Scriptures every day" to see if Paul was telling them the truth from God (Acts 17:11). So both by precept and example, Bible study is taught as a necessity in the life of a disciple.

There are some important characteristics to beneficial study of the Bible.

*Bible study must be consistent.* We should be doing some type of Bible study weekly or at least every other week. The lessons in many studies available today can easily be completed in a week.

*Bible study must be systematic.* We should have some system for it. A new Christian usually begins with a question-and-answer type of Bible study, which is one of the most effective types. Someone else has made up the questions and given the Scriptures to look up. This kind of study gets the new Christian into God's word. It directs the thinking of the student in a particular direction and is a useful tool for teaching biblical truth. It gives the new Christian something he can do for spiritual growth. It develops the habit of being systematic and regular in Bible study. It enables him to meet his needs through application. It teaches him to get information from the Bible. It familiarizes him with the entire Bible.

Many question-and-answer Bible studies are available today, from simple ones for new Christians to more difficult ones to challenge mature believers.[1]

For the growing disciple, the best kind of Bible study is the one commonly called chapter analysis.[2] In this type of study, the student goes through a book of the Bible chapter by chapter. Every disciple should be engaged in chapter analysis Bible study as a regular lifetime project, for this is the best way to get to know the word of God.

*Bible study must contain original investigation.* This means that we do not depend on the work of others, but commit ourselves to digging in the word of God on our own. We study the Bible, not books about the Bible. A question-and-answer Bible study provides an opportunity to make some discoveries and draw some conclusions, though there is quite a bit of direction given. Chapter analysis Bible study is not directed by specific questions or verses to consider, but there are some general questions that will guide original investigation.

1. What does the passage say? In your own words summarize or outline the passage under study. Do not try to interpret, but try to reproduce the thoughts of the writer in your own words.

2. What does the passage say that I do not understand? In this step list the problems that you have with the passage verse by verse. This does not necessarily mean that you will find answers for every problem, but it is a recognition that there are some things here which you do not understand.

3. What do other passages of Scripture say that help me understand this passage? This exercise is often called

finding cross-references, other Scriptures that say the same thing, or in some way help explain the verse in the passage under study. This is usually done with the help of a concordance.

*Bible study must include written reproduction.* We record what we have discovered in our searching. If a person does not record what he has studied, he has only read the Scriptures. The most effective and lasting way we can be instructed in righteousness is by writing down what God is teaching us.

*Bible study must have application to daily living.* It is useless to study the Bible if we are not going to apply its teachings. The most important question in Bible study must be, Lord, what do you want me to apply to my life from this portion that I am studying? A good question-and-answer study will include one or more questions that cause the student to consider how he should apply the truths he is studying. The person doing chapter analysis Bible study should ask himself this question: What does the passage say to me? This personal application is one of the most neglected parts of Bible study. Many people are satisfied with only an intellectual study of the Bible. True Bible study, as has often been emphasized in this book, requires personal application. If we are to be doers of the word of God, we must find portions of Scripture to apply.

Personal applications in Bible study can be written using the following procedure:

1. State in your own words the truth of the verse or passage that speaks to you.
2. Tell clearly how you have missed the mark that the verse or passage teaches.
3. Give a specific example of what you did wrong.
4. Write out how you will put into practice the teaching of the application verse or passage.

5. Set a date to check up on yourself to make sure you have carried out what you planned.

*Bible study must be "pass-on-able."* It must result in insights that could be shared meaningfully with another person, usually a younger Christian. The benefits of Bible study are not something that we keep for ourself, but we use them in our ministry to help others.

*Memorizing the Word of God*

The Scriptures are full of passages that indicate that God wants us to saturate our life with his word. Both the Old and New Testaments emphasize a relationship to God's word that can only come from Scripture memory. "These commandments that I give you today are to be upon your hearts" (Deuteronomy 6:6). "Keep my commands and you will live; guard my teachings as the apple of your eye. Bind them on your fingers; write them on the tablet of your heart" (Proverbs 7:2-3). "Let the word of Christ dwell in you richly as you teach and admonish one another with all wisdom" (Colossians 3:16). Since Scripture indicates without question that we are to memorize the word of God, we have only the options of obedience and disobedience.

Through Scripture memory you are able to grasp 100 percent of what you are learning, for you have it in your heart. It is probably the hardest method of intake, but it pays the greatest dividends spiritually. I have been memorizing Scripture for over twenty-five years and have found it to be the greatest blessing and strengthener in my life. Everyone can memorize if he wants to and will apply himself to it, but the spiritual battle will be tough. There are many excuses that people give as to why they can't memorize Scripture. The excuse "It involves too much discipline and effort" is perhaps the most truthful reason people give. The answer here is the matter of lordship. Is Jesus Christ really Lord of my life (see Chapter 2), and am I committed to live my life his way? If we are, then we will discipline ourself to do what he wants, and that includes Scripture memory.

It all boils down to the fact that Satan does not want us to memorize God's word and will bring a variety of excuses to mind. Ultimately it is a matter of what our priorities are going to be.

I met Mrs. Emma Reed a few years ago at a time when she had just started memorizing Scripture and had completed *The Topical Memory System.*[3] She quoted some verses from it without errors. She was continuing to memorize God's word on her own, and quoted some of those verses, again without errors. The interesting part of this story is that Mrs. Reed was 88 years old when she began memorizing Scripture!

*Advantages of Scripture memory.* The advantages of memorizing the word of God are many, and the benefits gained are exciting.

1. It increases our faith and trust in God. We begin to look at life more and more from his point of view. Paul wrote, "Your attitude should be the same as that of Christ Jesus" (Philippians 2:5). The memorized word of God enables us to have the mind of Christ at all times as we walk through life and thus builds our faith in his guidance and leading.

Bob Foster wrote the following about Scripture memory:

> There is a vast difference between "I have a verse," and, "It has me." The one can be the parrot-like repeating of words. . .the latter the transforming by the renewing of your mind.

> The daily habit of supplying the subconscious with God's material to chew upon. What I think about and meditate upon will eventually take on physical form and action. Get into the Book in some plan so the Book will get into you.[4]

2. It helps in general Christian growth. Peter wrote about this to new Christians. "Like newborn babies, crave pure spiritual milk, so that by it you may grow up in your salvation" (1 Peter 2:2). The same craving or desire should continue to be true as we mature in our faith.

3. It helps us to have victory over sin. The psalmist wrote, "I have hidden your word in my heart that I might not sin against you" (Psalm 119:11).

4. It has a cleansing effect. If we are to get rid of unclean thoughts which can lead to words and actions, we should substitute clean thoughts by concentrating on the word of God which we have memorized. We substitute thoughts instead of supressing them.

5. It increases our knowledge of the word of God and builds a doctrinal foundation for our life. It outlines the practical walk we are to have.

6. It is profitable for guidance. The psalmist has recorded God saying, "I will instruct you and teach you in the way you should go; I will counsel you and watch over you" (Psalm 32:8). One way God does that today is through his word.

7. It enables us to pray more effectively. Jesus tells us, "If you remain in me and my words remain in you, ask whatever you wish, and it will be given you" (John 15:7). It enhances our prayer life if we pray Scripture back to God. Memorizing key verses on prayer encourages us to pray and helps us remember how to pray. Jesus said, "Until now you have not asked for anything in my name. Ask

and you will receive, and your joy will be complete" (John 16:24). John wrote: "This is the assurance we have in approaching God: that if we ask anything according to his will, he hears us. And if we know that he hears us—whatever we ask—we know that we have what we asked of him" (1 John 5:14-15).

8. It helps us in our Bible study. We get some of our cross-references through memorized Scriptures. We are able to tie Scripture together and increase our understanding. The prophet wrote, "Precept must be upon precept, precept upon precept; line upon line, line upon line; here a little, and there a little" (Isaiah 28:10 KJV).

9. It helps us locate specific passages. When we memorize key verses, they enable us to turn to a whole passage on a particular teaching. Consider John 14:21, for example. "Whoever has my commands and obeys them, he is the one who loves me. He who loves me will be loved by my Father, and I too will love him and show myself to him." Knowing this verse enables us to turn to the passage to get further teaching on obeying the commands of God.

10. It helps us meditate on God's word. If we memorize the word of God, it enables the Holy Spirit to use these Scriptures to work in us. We may be reminded of what we are to say or do, or we may experience the power of the Holy Spirit in some other way. "Do not let this Book of the Law depart from your mouth; meditate on it day and night, so that you may be careful to do everything written in it. Then you will be prosperous and successful" (Joshua 1:8).

We will have something on which to meditate at times when it may not be possible to turn to a verse in the Bible.

11. It helps us worship God. When we hear a message on a subject or passage in which we have memorized verses, our interest is increased as we hear an explanation

and perhaps gain further understanding of that text.

In our private worship we are able to praise God through memorized praise passages of the Psalms (see Psalms 8, 9, 100, 117, 145, 146-150, and many others).

12. It helps us make good use of what might otherwise be wasted time, such as waiting in a long line at the grocery store. We may even find that a mind occupied with the word of God won't become impatient or angry.

13. It enables us to set an example for others to follow. Christians and non-Christians alike are always challenged by someone who knows the word of God. They realize that he has taken the time to memorize it and retain it. Challenge others with your example as Paul challenged others with these words: "Whatever you have learned or received or heard from me, or seen in me—put it into practice" (Philippians 4:9).

14. It enables us to witness effectively. Since witnessing is often not planned but comes on the spur of the moment, we should know the plan of salvation and the verses that present it. We are equipped for witnessing at any time if we have memorized key passages of God's word that are the best possible presentation of the good news of Jesus Christ and his salvation. Peter, for example, did not have the opportunity on the Day of Pentecost to read Joel's prophecy. Because he had those verses memorized, he could quote them to the crowd and build his sermon on them (see Acts 2:14-21).

Furthermore, the memorized word of God enables us to give the right answers to people who ask us about our faith. Peter, in his first letter to Christ's followers, advised them to "be prepared to give an answer to everyone who asks you to give the reason for the hope that you have" (1 Peter 3:15). We may not have the printed word of God available, but we are never without the memorized word.

15. It helps us in counseling others. The Prophet Isaiah wrote, "The Sovereign Lord has given me an instructed tongue, to know the word that sustains the weary" (Isaiah 50:4). We are able to counsel those who come to us ("sustain the weary") through the memorized word of God. The Holy Spirit will remind us of the needed verses for each individual.

I was on a plane once when a Christian man sat down next to me. After some preliminary conversation, he said to me, "I prayed that God would have me sit next to another Christian from whom I could get some counsel." As he told me of his needs, the Holy Spirit brought to mind some verses I had memorized, and I was able to counsel the man concerning his problems.

16. It helps in a public ministry. Anyone who is involved in a speaking or teaching ministry should be able to quote Scripture to make his points. This is what Peter did in his great sermon on the Day of Pentecost.

*General rules for Scripture memory*. Everyone can follow some guidelines for retentive memorization.

1. Start early in the week and day to learn a new verse. Ask the Holy Spirit to help you do it quickly and correctly.

2. Carry your verses with you at all times, preferably in a small pack. You can review memorized verses and learn new ones at various spare times during the day. A man or woman can review while waiting for an appointment. A student can review between classes.

3. Learn the topic and reference. Every verse has a topic that helps us remember and use it. Then learn the topic, reference, and first phrase. Add the second phrase to the topic, reference, and first phrase. Continue to add phrases until you have memorized the entire verse. Repeat the reference after quoting the complete verse.

4. Correct your mistakes immediately to maintain word perfection.

5. Ask someone to help you check out your newly-learned verses. Have a friend test you on all the verses that you are memorizing and reviewing.

6. Overlearn your verses. Repeat each verse six times a week for six weeks and it should be indelibly imprinted on your heart.

7. Use what you are memorizing in your ministry.

8. Set up a review system for those verses you memorized some time ago. Repeat them once a day for about six days or as many times as necessary to maintain quick and accurate recall.

*Meditating on the Word of God*

The final means of taking in the word of God is through meditation on it (see Figure 3). In God's design of the human hand, the thumb is able to touch the other four fingers. This is illustrative of the fact that we meditate on that which we hear, read, study, and memorize.

Meditation is simply reflecting on what you have on your mind. It is the process of contact with the Scriptures to the point that we understand their relationship to us and their application to our daily life.

In the opening psalm, blessing is promised the man who will not do wicked, sinful, and mocking things.

> Blessed is the man who does not walk in the counsel of the wicked or stand in the way of sinners or sit in the seat of mockers. But his delight is in the law of the Lord, and on his law he meditates day and night. He is like a tree planted by streams of water, which yields its fruit in season and whose leaf does not wither. Whatever he does prospers (Psalm 1:1-3).

The Scripture categorically states that the person who will meditate on God's word will be blessed, prosperous, and successful. Those are tremendous spiritual dividends. This makes meditation a very profitable exercise.

In meditation we take a verse we have heard, read, studied, or memorized, and begin mulling it over in our minds, to see what God wants to teach us through it. We concentrate on that particular verse and its message to us. Some ways to meditate on the word of God follow. These can be applied to verses you have heard, read, studied, or memorized.

1. Ask who, what, where, when, why, and how as you think about a particular verse, especially as it relates to you personally.

2. Think of a cross-reference for the verse you are meditating on. Then relate the teaching of the two verses in your mind.

3. In Bible reading, meditatively pray about the things God brings to your attention in your quiet time or other reading. How can they become part of your life?

4. Set aside a verse and call it "Victory-of-the-day verse," then meditate on it throughout the day. You will find it becoming a bulwark for you in temptation.

5. Meditate on a verse by emphasizing the different words in it and thinking about each emphasized word. For example, if you were meditating on Philippians 4:13 ("I can do everything through him who gives me strength."), you would emphasize the word *I*, then *can*, then *do*, and so on through the verse.

***

The man or woman who wants to be a disciple of the Lord Jesus Christ must commit himself wholly to every means of intake of the word of God on a regular basis: hearing, reading, studying, memorizing, and meditating on it.

---

NOTES:

1. The Navigators publish a number of excellent question-and-answer Bible studies that will be helpful to any Christian. These are the *Beginning with Christ Set* for new Christians, *Studies in Christian Living* or *Design for Discipleship* sets for growing disciples, and *The Life and Ministry of Jesus Christ* for advanced Bible students.
2. Detailed information on how to do chapter analysis Bible studies is available in two books published by NavPress: *A Layman's Guide to Interpreting the Bible* by Walter A. Henrichsen (which includes a large section on Bible study methods) and *The Navigator Bible Studies Handbook.* Both of these and the items in Note 1 are available from your local Christian bookstore.
3. *The Topical Memory System* is an effective memory course used by The Navigators for many years. It enables you to memorize the word of God and gives you suggestions on how to review all the verses you have memorized. The topics are vital ones to daily Christian living and discipleship, and should help in all aspects of your ministry. It is available from your local Christian bookstore.
4. Robert D. Foster, *The Challenge,* May 5, 1962 (Colorado Springs, Colorado).

# CHAPTER 7

# THE PRIMACY OF EVANGELISM

*A disciple has a heart for witnessing, gives his testimony clearly, and presents the gospel regularly with increasing skill.*

A disciple is always at the task of evangelism. He is constantly witnessing. He is always prepared to give an answer to anyone who asks him about his faith (see 1 Peter 3:15). At all times he is ready to communicate the gospel.

## Evangelism as a Lifestyle

The evangelism of Christian men and women in the early Church was characterized by three things.

1. They openly identified with Jesus Christ. Everywhere they went and in anything they did, they were not ashamed to be identified with the Savior. "Day after day, in the temple courts and from house to house, they never stopped teaching and proclaiming the good news that Jesus is the Christ" (Acts 5:42).

2. They demonstrated the fruits of the Spirit. There

was something in their lives that drew other people to them. Others, including their enemies, knew that they had been with Jesus. "When they saw the courage of Peter and John and realized that they were unschooled, ordinary men, they were astonished and they took note that these men had been with Jesus" (Acts 4:13). If we are to demonstrate that we are Jesus' disciples, we have to have the kind of life that will attract other people to the Savior.

3. They were actively seeking to influence other people toward Jesus Christ. That is evangelism. We read that right after the persecution that ended with the martyrdom of Stephen, the church was completely dispersed. But something happened when the church scattered to other areas of the Near East. Luke tells us, "Now those who had been scattered by the persecution in connection with Stephen traveled as far as Phoenicia, Cyprus and Antioch, telling the message only to Jews" (Acts 11:19). Then men from Cyprus and Cyrene began sharing the gospel with non-Jews, "and a great number of people believed and turned to the Lord" (Acts 11:21). These people were actively involved in evangelism, and saw the fruit of their ministry.

Evangelism is the key to disciplemaking and must be the cutting edge of any lasting ministry. In every ministry with which I have been involved, we always kept evangelism in the forefront. We could trust God to give us wisdom on how to handle the many spiritual babies he was going to give us, but we could never relax our efforts in evangelism.

I have known men who planned to evangelize for the first three months of the year, and then spend the other months discipling those who had been led to the Savior. The biblical pattern is involvement in both evangelism and discipling at the same time. Paul followed up and discipled the men he'd won to Christ, but he also kept on evangelizing. And so must we. Evangelism brings new life into a ministry.

When Ed Reis, a Navigator staff man, was ministering in London, England, God enabled him to reach some men at Lloyd's of London with the gospel. Lloyd's is the largest insurance market in the world. Ed began a study with a few of these men during the lunch hour. Several years later that ministry had grown to the point where hundreds of insurance brokers and underwriters were involved in Bible study and in weekly services at St. Helen's church near Lloyd's. This was all during the lunch hour! The reason for this growth? People were constantly being reached with the gospel. Those who began that ministry never lost their vision for evangelism.

Are people being added to your group because they are meeting Christ through the members of your group? It ought to be so. Evangelism must be the lifestyle of the disciple.

## The Importance of a Testimony

Successful evangelism generally begins with a well-prepared testimony, in which we share what Jesus Christ has done in our life. Participants in Evangelism Explosion clinics learn the following conversation, which is an effective opener for presenting one's testimony and the gospel.

"John, may I ask you a question?"

"Yes, you surely may."

"Have you come to the point in your spiritual life where you can say for certain that if you were to die tonight you would go to heaven?"

"No, I can't really say that."

"I appreciate that answer because there was a time when I didn't know how to get to heaven. I just assumed that nobody could know for certain. Then I discovered that there were people who did know that they were going to heaven. About this time I also found out that the Bible was written because God wants us to know we can go to heaven. 'I write these things to you...that you may know that you have eternal life.'"

"That's very interesting."

"Let me ask you another question which will bring everything into focus. Suppose you were to die tonight and stand before God and he were to say to you, 'Why should I let you into my heaven?' What would you say?"

"I guess what I'd probably say is that I tried to live a pretty good life, and I think that should be sufficient to enter heaven."

"In other words, you think that because you've tried to live up to the Ten Commandments and other things like that, God should let you into his heaven?"

"Yes, I'd say that's it."

"I understand exactly what you are saying. When I heard you answer the first question, I *thought* I had some good news for you, but as I hear your last answer, I *know* I have some good news for you. As a matter of fact, you are going to hear the greatest news you've ever heard in your life. May I share with you how I came to that point in my life where I knew that I had eternal life and how you can know it too?"

"Yes, I'd like to hear it."

"Most of my life I thought..."

*The Testimony as an Evangelistic Tool*

We cannot effectively communicate the gospel to others unless we share with them what Jesus Christ has done in our own life. We are the prime evidence that what we are talking about really works. No one can evangelize unless he has a personal relationship with Jesus Christ.

In 1957 I was in Morgan City, Louisiana, training counselors for a city-wide crusade. Morgan City is on the Atchafalaya River, one of the important centers for oil operations in the Gulf of Mexico, and was a strategic place for preaching the gospel. I suggested to the trainees that they learn how to communicate the gospel by an effective, sharp personal testimony. Curiously, 98 percent of the people claimed they had no testimony to offer. In analyzing the situation I discovered that they thought of a testimony as something spectacular in which a dramatic change occurred in a person. Since then I've found that many people, particularly those raised in Christian homes and Bible-believing churches, feel they have no testimony to share.

But the truth of the matter is that all of us have a testimony. It may not include a spectacular change, but there is change in everyone of us nevertheless. Any time the grace of God touches a life there is a story to tell.

In Evangelism Explosion training, we required that every person write out his or her testimony to be checked and graded by the instructor. The testimony has three basic points: first, what that person's life was like before he met the Savior; second, how that person came to know that he had eternal life; and third, the benefits of knowing Jesus Christ since conversion. Everyone should be able to write out a testimony like that.

Can you speak intelligently about your encounter with Jesus Christ? Many Christians can't—or won't. A disciple must. No matter where you are, you should be able to communicate the gospel of Jesus Christ through your testimony. A commitment to the primacy of evangelism is a must for the growing Christian disciple.

*Testimonies in Scripture*

The Bible gives us some clear testimonies. Two of Paul's sermons were nothing more than a retelling of how he met Jesus Christ. The first testimony was given to the mob of Jews that had just tried to lynch him. Paul began with what his life was like before he met the Lord in a dramatic way.

> The Jews all know the way I have lived ever since I was a child, from the beginning of my life in my own country, and also in Jerusalem. They have known me for a long time and can testify, if they are willing, that according to the strictest sect of our religion, I lived as a Pharisee.
>
> I too was convinced that I ought to do all that was possible to oppose the name of Jesus of Nazareth. And that is just what I did in Jerusalem. On the authority of the chief priests I put many of the saints in prison, and when they were put to death, I cast my vote against them. Many a time I went from one synagogue to another to have them punished, and I tried to force them to blaspheme. In my obsession against them, I even went to foreign cities to persecute them (Acts 26:4-5, 9-11).

Then Paul shared how he actually came to know the Savior.

> On one of these journeys I was going to Damascus with the authority and commission of the chief priests. About noon, O king, as I was on the road, I saw a light from heaven, brighter than the sun, blazing around me and my companions. We all fell to the ground, and I

> heard a voice saying to me in Aramaic, "Saul, Saul, why do you persecute me? It is hard for you to kick against the goads."
>
> Then I asked, "Who are you, Lord?"
>
> "I am Jesus, whom you are persecuting," the Lord replied. "Now get up and stand on your feet. I have appeared to you to appoint you as a servant and as a witness of what you have seen of me and what I will show you. I will rescue you from your own people and from the Gentiles. I am sending you to open their eyes and turn them from darkness to light, and from the power of Satan to God, so that they may receive forgiveness of sins and a place among those who are sanctified by faith in me" (Acts 26:12-18).

Finally, Paul told his audience what the Lord meant to him in his present life.

> So then, King Agrippa, I was not disobedient to the vision from heaven. First to those in Damascus, then to those in Jerusalem and in all Judea, and to the Gentiles also, I preached that they should repent and turn to God and prove their repentance by their deeds. That is why the Jews seized me in the temple courts and tried to kill me. But I have had God's help to this very day, and so I stand here and testify to small and great alike. I am saying nothing beyond what the prophets and Moses said would happen—that the Christ would suffer and, as the first to rise from the dead, would proclaim light to his own people and to the Gentiles (Acts 26:19-23).

Your testimony is your authority to speak about Christ and the gospel. We find an excellent example in the early Church. Peter and John had come to the temple in

Jerusalem to pray. On the way in, they had healed a man who had been born lame. After they had preached to the crowd that gathered, they were arrested and taken before the Sanhedrin, the ruling religious body of the Jews (see Acts 4:13-14).

Two things stand out here. The men in the Sanhedrin recognized that Peter and John had been with the Lord. They also saw the testimony of the former lame man, and had nothing to say. He had been lame and God had healed him through Peter and John. The testimony of two courageous lives and the testimony of a changed life were indeed powerful.

After the Sanhedrin threatened the two men, they were released. Peter and John went to prayer. Note what they asked for. "Now, Lord, consider their threats and enable your servants to speak your word with great boldness" (Acts 4:29). Boldness makes unembarrassed freedom of speech possible. In the Christian context, it means not being ashamed to talk about Jesus Christ. Peter and John were praying for freedom to proclaim the Gospel of Jesus Christ. By way of application, all of us need to pray for boldness to witness and testify to the Lord Jesus. Boldness which comes from God will enable us to share our testimony with anyone, and communicate the gospel to them.

God answered the prayer of Peter and John immediately. "After they prayed, the place where they were meeting was shaken. And they were all filled with the Holy Spirit and spoke the word of God boldly" (Acts 4:31). They went out and did what they were supposed to do in the power of the Holy Spirit, who enables us to witness and give our testimony effectively.

A well-told testimony can make a great impact on people. In our church we usually invited someone to give his or her testimony in the Sunday evening service. What about you? Could you share your testimony in such a way that it would be attractive to someone else and draw him or her to Christ?

## The Importance of Having a Plan

If the person with whom you have shared your testimony continues to be interested, you must now present the simple gospel story from the Scriptures so that he can come to a saving knowledge of Jesus Christ. For this you need a plan for a clear gospel presentation.

### *The Advantages of a Plan*

Use of a plan has several advantages to help you present the gospel intelligently.

1. It enables you to be prepared at all times to witness. You have a plan in mind; you are familiar with it and the Scriptures for it. You are able to answer anyone who wants to know how to come to Jesus Christ.

2. It enables you to go through a biblical presentation point by point without leaving anything out. You will have covered everything vital to that person's coming to Jesus Christ.

3. It serves as a set of tracks that provide direction. If the person with whom you are sharing the Lord takes off on a tangent, having a plan enables you to come back to where you ought to be after you have taken care of the diversion.

I had just started the presentation one time at Arizona State University and had shared the fact of sin with a college student. He said to me, "I don't believe in sin!"

I replied, "Now that's very interesting. What if we

took your thought life for the past two hours and somehow projected it on a large screen here on the campus. Would you like others to see what you have been thinking?"

He said, "No! Not at all!"

I asked, "Why not?" He was cornered and would not answer me. He knew he had thought some things that were evil, or sinful.

So I came back to the fact of sin and proceeded to the penalty of sin. My plan enabled me to stay right on track and present what the Bible teaches about salvation from God.

4. It is a transferable tool by which you can teach others to share Christ as well.

*Two Plans to Follow*

As a young Christian I learned a simple plan of gospel presentation and within a very short time was able to lead my first friend to the Lord. I want to suggest two plans you might use.

*The six main points of the gospel.* This is a simple plan using six words that represent six concepts and the Scriptures that teach each one. I have used this plan effectively for many years.

1. Disease—We begin with the fact that all of us are infected with the disease known as sin. It is a stark, irrefutable fact of human existence in this world. Use Romans 3:10-18 and 23.

2. Death—Sin leads to death, which is the penalty of sin. Use Romans 5:12 and 6:23.

3. Decree—Because God is righteous and holy, he cannot overlook our sins. Someone has to pay for them. Use Hebrews 9:27 and Exodus 34:6-7.

4. Deliverer—Someone else has paid for our sin and

is our deliverer from sins and their penalty. The penalty has already been paid by Jesus Christ on the cross of Calvary. Use Romans 5:8, Isaiah 53:6, and 1 Peter 2:24.

5. Declaration—The Bible further declares that this salvation cannot be earned, for it is a free gift from God to those who accept it by faith. Redemption is all of grace—absolutely free. Use Ephesians 2:8-9, Titus 3:5, and Romans 3:24.

6. Deliverance—Our deliverance comes when we receive Jesus Christ into our life by a prayer of commitment to him. Use Revelation 3:20, John 1:12, and Romans 10:9-10.

When a person understands what the Bible teaches and has received the Savior by faith, he needs to be assured that God indeed has saved him. So we need to conclude a successful gospel presentation by sharing with the convert some assurance verses. Some of the Scriptures that give this assurance are John 5:24, 1 John 5:11-13, John 10:28, Hebrews 7:25, and 1 Timothy 1:12.

*The Bridge Illustration.* Another effective gospel presentation that we have used in our Navigator ministries is called The Bridge to Life. When I was working with the military and meeting men in a snack bar, I would often take the napkin at the table and sketch out this illustration. I was talking with a man some years ago, when he suddenly reached into his wallet and pulled out a flimsy, worn piece of tissue paper. He asked, "Francis, do you remember this?" There was the diagram I had drawn for him years before. He had received Christ that same night and carried it with him as a reminder.

Following are the steps in the presentation of this plan. For each step, add important points and Scriptures to Figure 4 as you develop a picture of the relationship between God and man. Your completed illustration should look like that in Figure 5. Master this plan thoroughly so you will have an excellent tool in your hands for presenting the facts of the gospel.

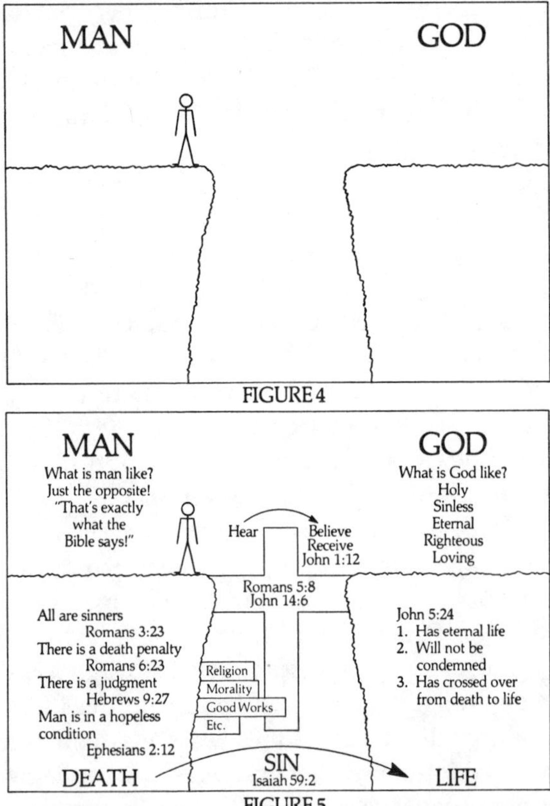


FIGURE 4

FIGURE 5

1. Begin by writing the word GOD on the right side of a sheet of paper and MAN on the left side. Then draw two cliffs with a chasm in between (see Figure 4). I often draw a little stick figure of a man on the left side.

2. Ask and write, "What is God like?" Write the answers given underneath the question. If the person with whom you are talking needs help, ask questions such as

these: "Do you think God is holy or unholy?" "Is he sinful or sinless?" "Is God temporal or is he eternal?" "Is he loving or hateful?"

3. Then ask, "What is man like?" as you write the question down. Any honest person will have to admit that man is just the opposite of God. History and contemporary society show man to be unholy, sinful, temporal, and hateful (plus opposites of other attributes of God that you might have listed).

To this point you have not used your Bible.

4. Now point out and discuss four facts about man presented in the Bible. As you do, write the facts on man's side of the chasm. Have the person you are witnessing to read Romans 3:23 ("For all have sinned and fall short of the glory of God"). Point out that there is a death penalty hanging over our head because of our sins.

Turn to Romans 6:23 ("For the wages of sin is death"). This death is an eternal separation from God.

The Bible also states that there is a judgment for our sins. Turn to Hebrews 9:27 ("Just as man is destined to die once, and after that to face judgment").

Conclude with Ephesians 2:12 ("Remember that at that time you were separate from Christ, excluded from citizenship in Israel and foreigners to the covenants of the promise, without hope and without God in the world").

The result of this is that man lives in death because sin separates him from God. "But your iniquities have separated you from your God; your sins have hidden his face from you, so that he will not hear" (Isaiah 59:2).

5. Ask what man does in an effort to build a bridge across his sin to God. You might suggest good works, morality ("I have kept the Golden Rule"), religion ("I go to church"), giving to charity, and many other things. List these efforts in the chasm. Point out that they all fall short

of bridging the chasm of separation. Base this point on Ephesians 2:8-9 ("For it is by grace you have been saved, through faith—and this not from yourselves, it is the gift of God—not by works, so that no one can boast"). The aim here is to show that man, through his own efforts, can't reach God.

6. Draw the cross in the chasm as the symbol that God has done something to bridge the chasm of separation between himself and man. Read Romans 5:8 ("But God demonstrates his own love for us in this: While we were still sinners, Christ died for us"). Emphasize that this is the only means by which we can get across to God. Then turn to John 14:6 ("Jesus answered, 'I am the way and the truth and the life. No one comes to the Father except through me' ").

7. Point out two elements which are necessary to actually cross over that chasm of separation. We must hear the message of God's salvation and provision, and we must believe or receive it personally. Read John 1:12 ("Yet to all who received him, to those who believed in his name, he gave the right to become children of God"). This is very important. In order for a person to come to God's side—to be saved—he has to hear the message of salvation, believe it, and receive Jesus Christ as his personal Savior and Lord.

8. Read John 5:24 ("I tell you the truth, whoever hears my word and believes him who sent me has eternal life and will not be condemned; he has crossed over from death to life"). Three tremendous results are seen here. The person who has heard the gospel, believed it, and received Jesus into his life has eternal life (a present possession). He no longer has any fear of condemnation (will not face judgment). He has found the bridge from death to life. He has these things because of the death of Jesus Christ on the cross for his sins.

At the conclusion of your presentation, ask the question, "Where are you?" This gives the individual you are talking with an opportunity to indicate where he feels he is. He could be totally on man's side of the chasm, still in a hopeless condition. He could have tried to get across the chasm in his own way. He may feel he is halfway across because he has heard the gospel. He could be anywhere.

*The Final Step*

Whichever plan you follow, do not leave anyone only with the facts of the gospel and his knowledge of where he stands with God. You need to bring him to the place of decision. His decision may be not to believe and receive Christ as Savior and Lord, but it is a decision nevertheless.

Many people are able to share Christ with others, but the problem often comes in getting them to receive the Lord. Disciples must know how to reap—how to lead people across the line, so to speak, of receiving Christ as their Savior.

We have to make sure the person with whom we have shared the gospel understands four basic things.

1. He must believe that he is a sinner.
2. He must know that judgment is sure to come and there is a spiritual penalty of death for sin.
3. He must believe that Jesus Christ came to this earth and died on the cross for *his* sins.
4. He must know that he needs to repent of his sins and put his trust and faith in Jesus Christ alone.

Ask, "Do these things make sense to you?" At this point you are beginning to change from presenting the facts, to asking the person what he is going to do about the facts he now says he understands.

The final question that should be asked is: "Would you like to receive this gift of eternal life?" If he says yes, then lead him in a prayer of confession of sin, belief in Jesus Christ, and acceptance of eternal life. If he says no, then either review the facts or consider the fleetingness of life and what happens when a person does not know Jesus Christ.

Another "reaping" approach I have used is to ask the prospect to turn to John 14:14 and read it. ("You may ask me for anything in my name, and I will do it.") Then I take out a piece of paper or a card and ask, "Would you like to know your sins are forgiven? Would you like your life to glorify God? Would you like eternal life?" We may list half a dozen things this person would like to have from God.

Then I say, "Why don't we pray for these things now? Jesus promises that if we ask for them in his name, he'll give them to us." So we pray, "Lord Jesus, forgive my sins and come into my life. Become my Savior and Lord and give me eternal life." This is reaping.

* * *

A true disciple of Jesus Christ must be involved in evangelism. If he isn't, then he is not a disciple but a convert who is still immature in vital areas of Christian discipleship. It is impossible to be a disciple without communicating the gospel to others.

---

NOTES: 1. This presentation is essentially what is done in Evangelism Explosion as an opener before going into the gospel presentation.

# CHAPTER 8

# THE CHURCH AND BODY LIFE

*A disciple attends church regularly to worship God, to have his spiritual needs met, and to make a contribution to the body of believers.*

If we trace the history of the church since the time of Christ, we find periods of unrest, falling away, and corruption. Yet God has always had a faithful remnant of disciples throughout the centuries. Today, as hundreds of years ago, the Scriptures call all Christ's disciples to be men and women who are involved in the church for the purpose of carrying out the Great Commission.

The first mention of the church in the New Testament was when Jesus asked his disciples who they thought he was. Peter made a great profession of faith.

> "You are the Christ, the Son of the living God." Jesus replied, "Blessed are you, Simon son of Jonah, for this was not revealed to you by man, but by my Father in heaven. And I tell you that you are Peter, and on this rock I will build my church, and the gates of Hades will not overcome it" (Matthew 16:16-18).

Jesus gave his followers the evangelistic task of reaching the world with the gospel. There is no question that the church was at the heart of this Great Commission, for the church which Jesus established is still actively engaged in carrying out the commission which he gave.

The central thrust of the Great Commission is the making of disciples. It is a continuous process in which men and women are converted to Jesus Christ, brought into the church, a living fellowship or body of responsible believers, and in time become reproductive Christians. This has been going on for nearly twenty centuries and is the main task of the church today, a task in which every disciple must find his place.

## THE CHURCH IN THE NEW TESTAMENT

The people of God are one throughout all ages, being those who believe God. They anticipated the Messiah in the Old Testament and trusted Jesus as Savior and Lord in the New. But the New Testament church is uniquely Jesus', for he is the one who formed it and has been building it on confessions similar to Peter's.

Between the resurrection and ascension of Jesus, there were over 500 believers in the Lord (see 1 Corinthians 15:6). These were men and women who were fully committed to the evangelistic task and were in absolute obedience to the Lord's command. He had told them to wait for the coming of the Holy Spirit, who was to give them the power to do what they had been commanded to do.

The promised Holy Spirit came on them on the Day of Pentecost (see Acts 2). The waiting disciples were filled with the Holy Spirit and were enabled to speak in the languages of the many visitors in Jerusalem. Immediately they began to witness, and they were heard and understood by Jewish people from many nations of the Mediterranean and Near East.

Their communication was so effective that it resulted in 3,000 professions of faith. These new believers were then baptized, identifying themselves with the church, and were added to the fellowship of those already believing.

What is important to note at this point is that the evangelistic task committed to us as Christian disciples falls short of its objective unless it relates new converts to local congregations of believers. New Christians must be associated with a local church so that the body of believers can be a source of nourishment for spiritual growth.

As soon as the new converts were incorporated into the church, their training in Christian living began. Luke records for us what happened to accomplish that training.

- They were instructed by the leadership of the church.
- They participated in the fellowship of the church.
- They joined with other believers in communion.
- They learned how to pray and devoted themselves to it.
- They observed the apostles as they preached and performed miracles.
- They realized their responsibility to one another in material things and had everything in common.
- They were generous in their sharing with those in need.
- They met together daily for worship in the temple.
- They gathered together in homes and ate with one another.
- They worshiped God with praise for what he had done for them.
- They had a good testimony in the city.

- They witnessed God's power as he added to their number daily (see Acts 2:42-47).

In time the new converts became witnesses and joined the mission of the church—carrying out the Great Commission by reproducing the whole process of making disciples. Figure 6 illustrates that process.[1]

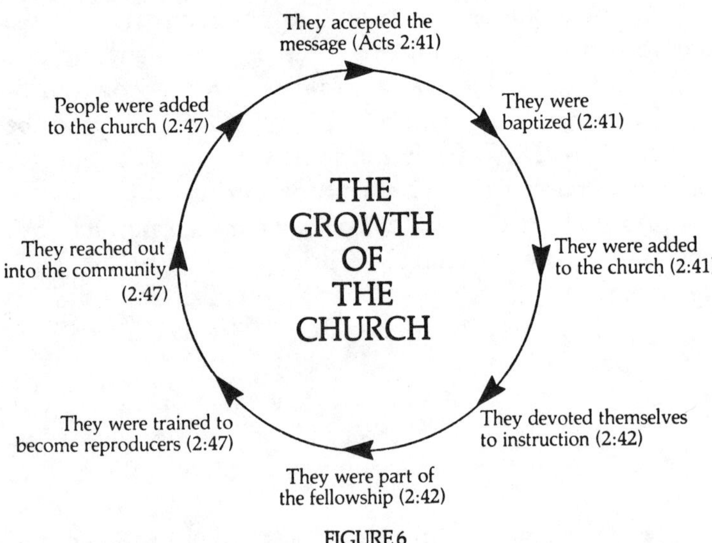


FIGURE 6

In one denomination in America in one year, there were some 2,000 churches which did not have a single convert to add to their number. In another denomination over 1,000 churches had no converts that year. We can see from the Acts record that the early Church recognized that its mission was to go out and make disciples. If a church is not doing this, then it is not doing what God intended his church to do. And the disciples in that church are not taking part in its ministry.

Vergil Gerber, one of today's leading authorities on church growth, has written:

> Thus evangelism in the New Testament does not stop with reaching people with the gospel, nor with the proclamation of the gospel, nor with public professions of faith in the gospel, nor even with relating them to the church through baptism and teaching.
>
> The evangelistic goal is not fulfilled until these new converts become reproducing Christians who complete the cycle and guarantee the continuous process of evangelism/church growth. The ultimate evangelistic goal in the New Testament, therefore, is two-fold: 1. to make responsible, reproducing Christians; 2. to make responsible, reproducing congregations.[2]

History tells us that within a single generation, the church of Jesus Christ had penetrated into all parts of the Roman Empire. The gospel was being preached, people were finding Christ as their Savior and Lord, and local churches were established. In the years that followed, the church grew even more rapidly in Roman society.

We see some evidence of this growth in the later writings of the Apostle Paul.

> We always thank God, the Father of our Lord Jesus Christ, when we pray for you, because we have heard of your faith in Christ Jesus and of the love you have for all the saints—the faith and love that spring from the hope that is stored up for you in heaven and that you have already heard about in the word of truth, the gospel that has come to you. All over the world this gospel is producing fruit and growing, just as it has been doing among you since the day you heard it and understood God's grace in all its truth (Colossians 1:3-6).

Justin Martyr, a philosopher who was won to faith in

Christ, wrote:

> There is not a single race of men, whether among barbarians or Greeks or by whatever name they may be called, of those who live in wagons or are called Nomads or of herdsmen living in tents, among whom prayers and thanksgiving are not offered through the name of the crucified Jesus to the Father and Maker of all things.[3]

The lawyer Tertullian recorded that "we are but of yesterday, and we have filled every place among you—cities, islands, fortresses, towns, marketplaces, the very camps, tribes, companies, palace, senate, and forum. We have left you only the temples."[4]

Historians tell us that by A.D. 323 approximately 10 percent of the Roman Empire's population, some 10 million out of about 100 million, had been won to the new faith. The gospel had also spread beyond the bounds of the empire into the Tigris and Euphrates valleys, along the shores of the Black Sea, into Armenia and Arabia, and even into India. The Mar Thoma Church of South India traces its roots all the way back to the Apostle Thomas, one of the Twelve.

Kenneth Scott Latourette, the great church historian, has written:

> Never in so short a time has any other religious faith, or, for that matter, any other set of ideas, religious, political, or economic, without the aid of physical force or of social or cultural prestige, achieved so commanding a position in such an important culture.[5]

God was founding his church in the world. His people, having been filled and empowered by the Spirit of

God, were following through with their commitment to Jesus Christ. Truly we can see, as Jesus had predicted, that "on this rock I will build my church, and the gates of Hades will not overcome it" (Matthew 16:18).

The church struggled through many persecutions, each of which ended with a period of peace before another outbreak came upon it. Not only did the church encounter difficulties from outside in the persecutions of the Roman government, but there were also constant struggles with false teaching and false doctrines. Peter had warned the church of this (see 2 Peter 2), but they arose nevertheless and the church at times succumbed to them. Throughout the centuries this internal attack has continued, and does so to the present day. Multitudes today are being drawn away by modern versions of ancient heresies.

Yet throughout the history of the church, there has always been a nucleus of people who have concentrated on the process of making disciples and trying to be obedient to the Great Commission. Many of those who were reached with the gospel, were discipled by godly men and women. Following their conversion some were ostracized and others were martyred for their faith. But the good news continued to spread during that time.

With the dawning of the Reformation in the early 16th century, the Holy Spirit moved in the lives of men such as Martin Luther and John Calvin and used them to bring the Scriptures to the forefront again. Luther and other men translated the Bible into the language of the people and enabled them to read the word of God in their own languages.

This return to the Scriptures gave rise to the modern missionary movement, as people, having been challenged by Christ's commission, were moved by the Holy Spirit to commit their lives to Christian service. William Carey went to India in 1792, giving birth to the forward thrust of modern missions. To this day the church is vitally ivolved in sending her members to the ends of the earth to carry the message of hope and salvation to a lost and dying world.

## The Leadership of the Church

Since God established his church to proclaim salvation, the leadership of the church is his responsibility. He must raise up men who will take the leadership positions in the church. Yet, as with many other biblical doctrines, the church too has a share in the responsibility to raise up leadership within itself that will serve and lead the church for years to come. Figure 7 illustrates the process and responsibilities of leadership.

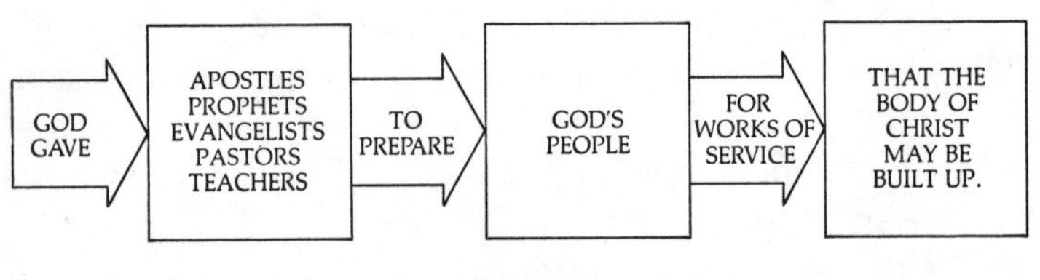


FIGURE 7

The Bible tells us that we are to submit to those in positions of leadership as unto the Lord. The writer to the Hebrews declared: "Obey your leaders and submit to their authority. They keep watch over you as men who must give an account. Obey them so that their work will be a joy, not a burden, for that would be of no advantage to you" (Hebrews 13:17). God has placed over us men who are responsible to keep us in the center of the will of God. They are responsible to rebuke us, to restrain us from sin, to restore us to fellowship, and to help us avoid false doctrines and teachings.

Because of the service of leaders in the church, we are to hold them in high respect. Paul wrote: "Now we ask you, brothers, to respect those who work hard among you, who are over you in the Lord and who admonish you. Hold them in the highest regard in love because of their work" (1 Thessalonians 5:12-13). Our responsibility is to respect the leaders of the church whom God has placed over us.

Additional teaching on leadership is given to us by Paul. He wrote to the Ephesians:

> It was he who gave some to be apostles, some to be prophets, some to be evangelists, and some to be pastors and teachers, to prepare God's people for works of service, so that the body of Christ may be built up until we all reach unity in the faith and in the knowledge of the Son of God and become mature, attaining to the whole measure of the fullness of Christ (Ephesians 4:11-13).

God has provided responsible leadership for his church. The original leaders were the apostles. These men were given the responsibility of carrying out the Great Commission. They have passed that responsibility on to others.

Another type of leadership is that of prophet. The New Testament prophet is not one who foretells the future, but rather one who tells forth the word of God. His responsibility is to communicate the word of God and make sure that the people understand it.

Another type of leader is the evangelist. This is a person who has been anointed by God with the special responsibility of communicating the message of the gospel to many people. A notable example of an evangelist is Billy Graham, who has been used of God around the world in leading many people to the Savior through his preaching.

A leader in the local church is the pastor-teacher who shepherds the people. These are men who have taken the responsibility of nurturing and ministering to a local congregation.

There are some men and women of God who are specially gifted to teach the word of God to others. Often they are speakers at conferences across the nation. They are able to teach the Scriptures in such a way that the lives of the people listening are changed. Our seminaries and other training institutions are the means by which able men of God teach and train young men and women to become faithful servants of Christ and the leaders of tomorrow.

Many of us have had the privilege in our local churches of sitting at the feet of men of God who have taught us many things and prepared us for our own ministry of leadership.

The Bible also tells us that other kinds of leadership have been provided for the local church. Elders are responsible for the purity of the gospel; they are guardians of the faith. They have been given the responsibility to make sure that the doctrines and truths taught by others in the church are the pure truth of the word of God. Paul describes the qualifications of an elder, sometimes referred to as an overseer or bishop, in 1 Timothy 3:1-7 and Titus 1:6-9.

God also established the position of deacon for the local church. The qualifications of these men are spelled out for us in their original selection (see Acts 6:3) and by the Apostle Paul (see 1 Timothy 3:8-12). Their responsibilities include the care of widows and the administration of financial responsibilities of the local church.

When I consider how God raises up leaders for his church, I cannot help but think of my own experience. I received Christ as my Savior when I was seventeen years old. Less than a month later God began speaking to me about considering the full-time ministry. I responded to that and began looking to God over the years for his leadership and direction toward the ministry he had for me.

It has been a great privilege for me to serve Jesus Christ, and to have the joy of ministering to men and watching God use that ministry in their lives. These men have grown to places of leadership in the church and have been serving Jesus Christ faithfully in the process of building disciples through home Bible studies and in working with other men on an individual basis.

## Church Membership

As a Christian, you have certain responsibilities toward God and toward other believers. When you received Jesus Christ as Savior and Lord, you became a member of the universal, or "invisible," church. You belong to "the family of believers" (Galatians 6:10) and are part of the body of Christ.

Since we belong to Jesus Christ and his universal church, we have the responsibility of obeying him and joining a local manifestation of that body. The writer to the Hebrews stated, "Let us not give up meeting together, as some are in the habit of doing, but let us encourage one another—and all the more as you see the day approaching" (Hebrews 10:25).

*Guidelines for Choosing a Church*

Church membership is not to be entered into lightly. The church we choose should minister to us as Christ's disciples. It should give us the greatest opportunities of service, where we can best exercise our spiritual gifts. We must prayerfully seek a church where these conditions are found.

More specific guidelines for selecting a church include the following:

*The church should provide the greatest opportunity for personal and family growth.* We need to be taught and trained from the time of our spiritual rebirth to the time of our physical death.

*The church should offer an opportunity to be involved in carrying out the Great Commission.* We need to be involved in the proclamation of the gospel to those who do not know Jesus Christ.

*The church must provide an opportunity for its members to glorify God and to worship him.* We do not go to church to hear and evaluate a sermon; we go to church to worship almighty God.

There are two basic criteria by which we can determine if we have really worshiped God. Was I encouraged and strengthened in my devotion to Christ? Did I spend some time worshiping the Lord by reflecting on who he is? Did I respond to the ministry of the word of God with the desire to obey what God has said to me?

Second, as I walk out of that church building or meeting place, do I have a desire to communicate the good news of Jesus to others? Am I concerned with the salvation of other men and women?

*The church must provide a place and opportunity for fellowship for its members.* All of us have experienced the joys and blessings of the communion that takes place as

Christians get together in true biblical fellowship. As Christian disciples we should look forward to the next contact we have with believing friends and members of our church. We have seen how the social life of the early Church was centered around the gathering together of the believers.

*The church must provide a place for strengthening our faith.* It must ground us in the doctrines of our faith. Godly teachers explain the principles and truths of the word of God to us. As we are joined together with others in times of prayer, sharing of testimonies, preaching, teaching, and fellowship, we are strengthened in our faith and in our walk with the Lord.

It has been a great joy to me as a husband and father to be in a church where my whole family can be involved. I am thankful for the opportunities for spiritual growth that the church has provided for my children, reinforcing what we have been teaching them in the home. They are growing and maturing in Christ and the foundation of their lives has been greatly strengthened by godly Sunday school teachers and others who have ministered to them.

*The church should provide opportunities for Christian service.* God allows us to remain in the world so that we might serve others and reach out to them with the gospel. That is the plan he has ordained for his people. One opportunity for service in a church may be to fill one of the positions of leadership discussed earlier.

*The church must provide a means for channeling our finances into the Lord's work.* The Scriptures teach that we are to give our tithe for the furtherance of the ministry of God's church. In addition to our tithe, we are also taught to give to the Lord offerings as he has prospered us.

Giving can also be a giving of time and work. It could be volunteering to see that bulletins are folded and stuffed, or that a public address system is properly installed. Giving is one of the greatest joys that a disciple can have.

As we prayerfully make a decision concerning which church to become involved in, we must remember that we will not find a perfect church. Billy Graham cautions us against such an expectation.

> It has been said, "In practical terms this membership of the body of Christ must actually mean membership of some local manifestation of his body in the church."
>
> It is true that we are not talking about the great universal church now, but the local church, the one in your own community, of whose many imperfections and shortcomings you may be well aware. But we must remember that perfection does not exist among human beings, and the institutions they create for the greater glory of God are filled with these selfsame flaws. Jesus is the only perfect Man who ever lived. The rest of us are at best but repentant sinners, try as we may to follow his magnificent example; and the church is but turning a blind eye toward itself when it claims infallibility or perfection for itself or any of its members.
>
> When Jesus founded the church, he intended his followers to join it and remain faithful to it.[6]

* * *

If you have committed yourself to being one of Christ's 20th-century disciples, then associate yourself with a local congregation. But be sure it is a church that is committed to carrying out the Great Commission. When you join such a fellowship, you will reap all the benefits that such membership affords you as a follower of Jesus Christ. You need the church and the church needs you.

NOTES:

1. This illustration is adapted from Vergil Gerber, *God's Way to Keep a Church Going and Growing* (Glendale, California: Regal Books, 1973), p. 15.
2. Ibid., p. 18.
3. As quoted by Ernest Trice Thompson, *Through the Ages: A History of the Christian Church* (Richmond, Virginia: The CLC Press, 1965), pp. 20-21.
4. Ibid., p. 21.
5. Kenneth Scott Latourette, *A History of the Expansion of Christianity*, Vol. 1, *The First Five Centuries* (New York and London: Harper & Row, Publishers, Incorporated, 1937), p. 112.
6. Billy Graham, *Peace with God* (New York: Pocket Books, 1965), pp. 163-164.

CHAPTER

# 9

# CHRISTIAN FELLOWSHIP

*A disciple fellowships regularly with other believers, displaying love and unity.*

Christian fellowship is vitally related to the local church (see Chapter 7). For many Christians the only fellowship they experience is provided by their local congregation. Others, however, find fellowship in both their church and in home Bible study groups or other special groups that meet on a regular basis. Christian fellowship is an absolute necessity in the life of every believer, whether it is totally tied to a local church or includes other interchurch activities.

Fellowship is carried on wherever a body of believers gathers together. Whenever a Christian is isolated from others who have a similar relationship with Jesus Christ, there is something missing from his or her life. Even though that person may have fellowship with Christ through the word and prayer, the mutual encouragement and strengthening that comes from association with other believers in the Lord is missing.

## THE MEANING OF THE WORD FELLOWSHIP

It is important that we understand the meaning of the word *fellowship* because it is the key to understanding what the biblical concept of Christian fellowship is. The Greek term *koinonia* is used throughout the Scriptures and is translated into English consistently as "fellowship." *Koinonia* means "sharing in something with someone."[1] John Stott explains the implications of the word well.

> A careful study of the New Testament use of this word-group indicates that Christian *koinonia* or "commonness" takes three forms.
>
> First and foremost, there is what we share in together, our common Christian inheritance. Indeed this is the fundamental meaning of the word. . . .
>
> In particular, we share in the saving grace of the three persons of the Trinity. Thus, through the witness of the apostles we come to have fellowship with them, and their fellowship is "with the Father and with his Son Jesus Christ." Indeed, our "fellowship with one another" is dependent on our "fellowship with him." . . .
>
> But fellowship is more than what we share *in* together. There is also and secondly, what we share *out* together. For *koinonia* in the New Testament concerns not only what we possess but what we do together, not only our common inheritance but also our common service. . . .
>
> The gospel is not the only treasure, however, which Christians have to share out together. Another is our material possessions. Rich people are to be especially *koinonikos*, "generous," and all Christians are told not to neglect *koinonia*, but rather to "contribute (*koinoneo*) to the needs of the saints." . . .

> Let me now summarize the threefold aspect which *koinonia* wears in the New Testament. It speaks of our common inheritance (what we share in together), of our co-operative service (what we share out together), and of our reciprocal responsibility (what we share with one another). In the first we are receiving together, in the second we are giving together, while in the third there is mutual give and take.[2]

Each one of us as a Christian has much to share with other fellow believers. If we were to make a list, it would be endless. We should share our daily experiences with Jesus Christ' guidance and forgiveness, the ministry of helping others grow in Christ, our efforts in evangelism, and insights on teaching Sunday school classes.

One of the blessings of our fellowship together is that as we share our walk with Jesus Christ, we can encourage other believers who may be going through some problems we have experienced. In fact, the Apostle Paul taught that God "comforts us in all our troubles, so that we can comfort those in any trouble with the comfort we ourselves have received from God" (2 Corinthians 1:4).

A beautiful illustration of fellowship may be seen in the experience of the early Church. In Chapter 7 we looked at a passage from Acts which is a description of the training or instruction new converts received within the local body of believers (see Acts 2:42-47). That same passage gives an excellent example of true fellowship.

God was certainly honored in the early Church as the believers displayed love and unity. Glory comes to God from this kind of fellowship, for out of it is born a living, powerful witness, that causes men and women to fall to their knees and acknowledge Jesus Christ as Savior and Lord of their life.

## The Basis of Christian Fellowship

The Apostle John stated that the source of fellowship was a relationship with the Lord. "We proclaim to you what we have seen and heard, so that you also may have fellowship with us. And our fellowship is with the Father and with his Son, Jesus Christ" (1 John 1:3). John knew what it was to have an intimate relationship with the Lord. He had heard him, seen him, and even touched him (see 1 John 1:1). During Jesus' ministry, John had a close relationship with Jesus; he had talked with him and had shared his heart with him.

John then invited his readers to join with him in that fellowship with Jesus. The basis of Christian fellowship is the relationship that we individually have with God through Jesus Christ. It is only because of that relationship that we can have fellowship with one another within the body of Christ. And because the other person also has a dynamic relationship with the Lord, we profit from it and experience the encouragement and mutual sharing that is so necessary for all of us.

It is impossible for Christians to have true biblical fellowship with people who do not know Jesus Christ. Even though they may be our relatives and friends, dearly loved and respected by us, we cannot experience the biblical fellowship that we need unless they know Jesus Christ personally.

Love and unity also are absolute necessities if there is going to be true biblical fellowship. Paul wrote to one of his churches, "If you have any encouragement from being united with Christ, if any comfort from his love, if any fellowship with the Spirit, if any tenderness and compassion, then make my joy complete by being like-minded, having the same love, being one in spirit and purpose"

(Philippians 2:1-2). For true fellowship to take place, there must be love and unity among the participants. There is no disunity or lack of love when the Holy Spirit is in control. When a group of Christians have surrendered to the will of God and are letting the Holy Spirit control their lives and govern their situations, the result will be Christian fellowship.

During my days as a single man, I lived with four other men in a Navigator home. The purpose of living together was to receive training from one of the men in ministry skills and character development. We developed some difficulties in that home caused by unbroken spirits before the Lord and deep problems of pride. The Lord spoke to me through Ephesians 4:3, and the words stood out to me like a direct command: "Francis, make every effort to keep the unity of the Spirit through the bond of peace." It was a real revelation to me, for I had to ask myself, "Am I a cancer in the midst of the body of Christ, causing disruption? Or am I a unifier and peacemaker?" In our relationships with other Christians we have to love one another and maintain the unity of the Holy Spirit.

In his last ministry to the disciples before the cross, Jesus told them, "A new commandment I give you: Love one another. As I have loved you, so you must love one another. All men will know that you are my disciples if you love one another" (John 13:34-35).

This love of which Jesus was speaking includes putting the interests and concerns of other people ahead of ours. One of the practical ways in which this may be done is to call a friend, especially one who might be undergoing some testings or difficulties. Visit with him for a while, then share a verse of Scripture as a word of encouragement and assure him that you are praying for him. Share some of the victories that God is giving you personally. These few moments spent on the phone with a Christian brother will involve you in real fellowship.

Many times while I was working with my church in Fort Lauderdale, I would stop in the other offices in the church and give a word of encouragement and appreciation to the secretaries and others who worked there. I would share a verse of Scripture with them and let them know that I was concerned for them, and that they were having a vital ministry in the church. A few moments spent in such a way are part of true Christian fellowship.

## THREE BASIC ELEMENTS OF BIBLICAL FELLOWSHIP

These elements must be present if true fellowship is to take place among Christians.

### *Fellowship Must Include a Challenge to Grow*

Whenever a group of Christians meets together for Bible study, a time of prayer, or a discussion of the Scriptures, there must be a challenge to growth that each person can respond to. A Bible study may emphasize a needed personal application for one person, and challenge another to study a subject in greater depth. A time of prayer may challenge someone to memorize verses concerning prayer.

Two couples became regulars in our Bible study in Fort Lauderdale. Both couples were relatively young in their Christian experience. They were greatly encouraged by the warmth and friendliness of every person in the group, by the mutual sharing of the word of God, and by the fact that they could enter into the discussion. They were strengthened in their relationship to the Lord, and as a result of that fellowship continued to grow in Jesus Christ.

*Fellowship Must Involve Sharing Jesus Christ with One Another*

This sharing does not necessarily have to be evangelistic, but it can be. We could be involved in a Bible study in which there are some non-Christians. Because of the sharing of experiences each believer has had with the Savior, the unbelievers may be challenged to consider him as their Savior and Lord.

Sharing of Christ between Christians includes victories and joys of submission and obedience to the word of God. It means sharing the joy of knowing that we are walking in the center of his will. It is sharing what we are getting out of our quiet time each morning. It is telling other believers of the blessings we have received, the provision God has made for our needs, and his marvelous answers to our prayers.

A young woman joined one of our evening Bible studies in Miami. After one evening with that group, she came to me and said, "Francis, this is what I have been looking for for a long time." She found genuine fellowship with our group because we were discussing the word of God and Christians were sharing what Jesus meant to them in their daily experience. She left with a great joy in her heart because of finding a fellowship that met her needs.

*Fellowship Must Motivate All Those Present to Consistent Outreach*

If we have experienced the type of fellowship that has challenged us to grow and in which Christ has been shared, a natural outgrowth should be the desire to share him with others who do not know him.

Perhaps you have experienced the excitement of seeing people come to Christ and then become involved in a challenging fellowship with other believers. As a result of that exposure, they have been getting into God's word and in a short while become concerned for their friends who are still outside of Christ. They want them to come to know the Savior as they have done. And many of these people who have never received training do reach out and lead their friends and relatives to Jesus.

### *Biblical Fellowship Illustrated*

The story of Jesus meeting two men on the way to Emmaus after his resurrection is a good illustration of Christian fellowship.

On the day of resurrection, two of Jesus' disciples, not knowing that Jesus had risen from the dead, were walking toward the village of Emmaus, seven miles from Jerusalem. Luke tells us that they were sad because they thought the one in whom they had placed all their hopes was now dead.

Jesus joined them, but did not reveal himself to them. As they talked, Jesus began to teach them what the Scriptures had to say about the Messiah, and helped them understand all the events of the past week. He revealed himself to them after they reached the village, then vanished from their sight. "They asked each other, 'Were not our hearts burning within us while he talked with us on the road and opened the Scriptures to us?' " (Luke 24:32).

The word of God had been opened up to them and their response was warm and receptive. They were encouraged and greatly strengthened in their relationship with the living God. The fellowship with Jesus and with one another challenged them to growth.

### *Misconceptions about Fellowship*

In our society today there are some misconceptions about what fellowship really is. Many things Christians do are not fellowship. For example, a group of men may get together and go fishing or camping. Or several couples may go to a concert together. Some may go and visit Christian friends, play some games, and eat a meal.

Unless the three basic elements are present in the gathering together of believers, it does not qualify as biblical fellowship. There must be a challenge to grow in Christ, there must be the sharing of Jesus with one another, and there must be some outreach or plans for outreach made concerning those without Christ. If these things don't take place when Christians are with one another, then it is best to call that gathering companionship.

I asked the members of a Bible study group to evaluate their lives in terms of time spent in the word, prayer, fellowship, and witnessing. Almost everyone thought they were succeeding under fellowship, but were having some difficulty with one or all of the others.

If we are going to do what the Bible defines as fellowship, then it will require some discipline on our part. How tragic it is that so many believers are seeking genuine Christian fellowship, but are then stunted in their growth because what they have found is not really fellowship but Christian companionship.

## The Results of Biblical Fellowship

Several things result when Christians have real fellowship with one another. Fellowship results in needed encouragement, necessary correction, and becoming the kind of person God wants us to become.

### *Fellowship Results in Encouragement*

All of us get tired and discouraged, and need encouragement from others. King David had a word of encouragement for his son Solomon. "Be strong and courageous, and do the work. Do not be afraid or discouraged, for the Lord God, my God, is with you. He will not fail you or forsake you until all the work for the service of the temple of the Lord is finished" (1 Chronicles 28:20).

Whenever our parents, leaders, or those over us speak like that, we are greatly encouraged. For all of us need encouragement, and the place to receive it is in the fellowship to which we belong. The right word at the right time from a friend will certainly renew us inwardly. That is the way the Spirit of God ministers to us. I have at times gone away from a close fellowship greatly encouraged, though no one knew that they had been used by God in that way.

Another source of encouragement is from God himself through his word as it is shared with us. For example, a friend may share a verse which reminds us of God's concern: "So do not fear, for I am with you; do not be dismayed, for I am your God. I will strengthen you and help you; I will uphold you with my righteous right hand" (Isaiah 41:10).

*Fellowship Involves Correction*

Fellowship provides the correction necessary for our spiritual growth. We will never be able to live our Christian life without the correction that is provided for us through fellowship with other believers. When a person is without fellowship, he may not realize he is deviating from the straight and narrow. The writer to the Hebrews wrote: "See to it, brothers, that none of you has a sinful, unbelieving heart that turns away from the living God. But encourage one another daily, as long as it is called Today, so that none of you may be hardened by sin's deceitfulness" (Hebrews 3:12-13).

Sin always shows its effects in our life. When these effects are visible to others in our fellowship who know the Lord, they are able to help us. They can minister to us a word of correction or rebuke and help us recognize how important it is to deal with such things. We need humility to recognize our own needs and to submit to others.

I was on a visitation team which called on a woman who was having a difficult time in her Christian experience and who had not been attending church. As we opened up God's word to her, shared some promises with her, and prayed together, she saw what was lacking in her life. She was out of fellowship with other believers and was not receiving from them. She needed to have the humility to be able to receive from others, for that is what God intended for her and other believers in Christian fellowship.

Is it possible to survive and grow spiritually without Christian fellowship? Basically, no. It is one of the vital necessities in our life. But there have been situations where by God's grace, people have been able to go for long periods of time without the fellowship of others who know the Lord. This was true, for example, among the Christian prisoners-of-war in North Vietnam. Some missionaries have worked among tribes in remote areas where they had no contact with fellow Christians for three or four years. But these times are temporary. The prisoners-of-war were finally released, and missionaries come home on furlough regularly. Today, because of radio and small airplanes that supply remote missionary bases, they are able to have fellowship on a regular basis.

In The Navigators we generally send our people overseas in teams of at least two couples. That is because of this teaching of Scripture: "Two are better than one, because they have a good return for their work: If one falls down, his friend can help him up. But pity the man who falls and has no one to help him up!" (Ecclesiastes 4:9-10)

We need other Christians to encourage and correct us in our Christian life if we are to survive in this hostile world.

*Fellowship Helps Us Become What We Ought to Be*

What kind of a person are you becoming? We can get a good idea of the answer by taking a good look at those with whom we fellowship. Solomon wrote long ago, "He who walks with the wise grows wise, but a companion of fools suffers harm" (Proverbs 13:20).

If you are in mutual communion and fellowship with others who know the Savior and who are committed to his lordship, then you will grow and increase in the depth of your relationship with Jesus Christ and with one another. Fellowship is as important to our spiritual life as exercise is to our physical body. We *must* have fellowship with those of like precious faith.

Why are you walking with God today? Why are you in the word of God today? For me it was because at a critical time in my Christian experience God led me to a warm fellowship of believers. This was a group of young men my age in the Navy who loved Jesus Christ, who were interested in learning what his word had to say, who wanted their lives governed by it, and who wanted to learn to live according to the will of God. This group of sailors was under way in Bible study, was memorizing Scripture, was praying together, and as a result was experiencing true biblical fellowship. God helped me in those early days of my Christian experience to grow through association with that fellowship.

For you, a source of stimulating fellowship may be the local church. Multitudes of Christians have been nurtured and cared for within a body of believers. It is important for the local church and its leadership to be committed to helping the people under their care grow in the Lord and experience the fellowship that the Bible calls all believers to. Fellowship is a vital necessity for the people of God.

* * *

Make fellowship an integral part of your life. Make sure it is Christ-centered and motivates you to reach out to those around you who do not know the Savior. It must be one that encourages you, provides correction when you need it, and helps you become the person Christ intended and enables you to be.

---

NOTES: 1. J. D. Douglas, ed., *The New Bible Dictionary* (Grand Rapids, Michigan: William B. Eerdmans Publishing Company, 1962), p. 245.

2. John R. W. Stott, *One People* (Downers Grove, Illinois: InterVarsity Press, 1968), pp. 75-81.

# CHAPTER 10
# THE DISCIPLE IS A SERVANT

*A disciple demonstrates a servant heart by helping others in practical ways.*

Dr. V. Raymond Edman, late president of Wheaton College, one of the great Christian schools in America, once said, "Our job is not to train leaders, but to train servants." Throughout its history Wheaton has sent many servants of the cross into the fields of the world. That's a tremendous objective for a school, for the world has all too few servants. Many people aspire to leadership, to fame, and to success, but very few aspire to servanthood.

The Bible emphasizes serving others. A great example is that of Jesus as he washed the feet of his disciples. He was a matchless demonstration of love and servanthood in that he came to die for the sins of men. John explained that "this is how we know what love is: Jesus Christ laid down his life for us. And we ought to lay down our lives for our brothers" (1 John 3:16).

This emphasis on servanthood is contrary to the practice of most secular leadership. In most cases those in high management demand service from others. That's the way things are done in our world. But when Jesus came, he reversed the direction of service without giving up his leadership. In fact he enhanced his leadership because of his service.

Jesus taught the disciples to be servants. During a discussion on who should be the greatest, he told them:

> You know that the rulers of the Gentiles lord it over them, and their high officials exercise authority over them. Not so with you. Instead, whoever wants to become great among you must be your servant, and whoever wants to be first must be your slave—just as the Son of Man did not come to be served, but to serve, and to give his life as a ransom for many (Matthew 20:25-28).

This teaching of leadership by serving continues to have an unfamiliar ring in an age that calls for us to do everything we can to climb to the top. The Bible teaches that to lead is to serve. We may recognize the truth of this concept and respond with a positive attitude. The problem, however, arises in doing it day to day.

Since servanthood is taught in the Bible as part of being a disciple of Jesus Christ, we want to examine what a servant is, look at some characteristics of a servant, and discover how we can be servants practically. The chapter concludes with a few thoughts about the blessings of a life of servanthood.

## What Is a Servant?

Paul introduced himself to the church in Rome as a servant first, then an apostle. "Paul, a servant of Christ Jesus, called to be an apostle and set apart for the gospel of God" (Romans 1:1). Apostleship was an office, but servanthood deals with people. One of the greatest honors that anyone could grant us would be to call us a servant of Christ. Throughout the history of the church, godly men and women have often been designated by expressions such as "a true servant of the Lord."

LeRoy Eims, International Ministry Representative for The Navigators, has written:

> Jesus gave us the basic summary of his life: "For even the Son of man came not to be ministered unto, but to minister, and to give his life a ransom for many" (Mark 10:45). He was among us as one who served (see Luke 22:27).
>
> Today it is not possible for us to serve the Lord by taking a sacrificial animal to the side of a hill, kindling a fire, and presenting it to him. To serve God we must serve others, as Jesus did. The leader must offer his own life on the altar of God to be consumed in the flame of God's love, in service to others.[1]

Servanthood deals with people, and at heart is our willingness to go out of our way to meet a need in someone's life, to do something that needs to be done.

That's why I believe God is using Dr. James Kennedy so much. He is where he is today because he has been the greater servant of others in the church and in the Christian world.

Dr. Kennedy has many responsibilities. He is the founder and president of Evangelism Explosion. He is the head of Coral Ridge Ministries. He serves on the Board of Directors of Westminster Academy. He is involved in radio and television ministries. But he places a high priority on involvement in the evangelism training programs for the laymen of the church. Every week he leads a team of three people in calling in homes. Dr. Kennedy serves his people by teaching them and helping them become disciples.

The term *servant*, according to the Scriptures, cannot easily be tied down to one specific definition. Rather, it is used to mean a variety of things. Many times a servant is also called a slave. The Hebrews in the Old Testament had two types of servants or slaves, those bought and those taken in wars. In that society people were also able to sell themselves to pay their debts.

In the Bible entire nations were required to serve their king or those who conquered them. So Israel is spoken of as a servant to her king and the Syrians are referred to as the servants of King David. Depending on the course of history, the Israelites served the Philistines, and on other occasions the Philistines served Israel.

The person who dedicates himself to the service of another by his own choice of will is also considered a servant. So we find that Joshua became the servant of Moses, Elisha became the servant of Elijah, and the disciples became servants of Christ. "For we do not preach ourselves, but Jesus Christ as Lord, and ourselves as your servants for Jesus' sake" (2 Corinthians 4:5). The Apostle Paul chose to be a servant. "Though I am free and belong to no man, I make myself a slave to everyone, to win as many as possible" (1 Corinthians 9:19). In all of these cases these men were eventually exalted to higher positions.

Perhaps the most common reference in the Scriptures is to servants of the Lord. First, there are the faithful and godly persons who have been redeemed from sin and are now serving God in righteousness and holiness (see Romans 6:17-18). Second, a person who serves God in a particular function or calling is designated a servant of God. Jesus Christ, for example, is called God's servant prophetically (see Isaiah 53:11). Third, the expression "servant of God" may be applied to a person whom God uses to perform his will in a particular mercy or judgment. Moses, for example, is called the servant of God seventeen times in the Scriptures, and David is so designated some twenty-four times.

Putting these biblical teachings together, we discover that a servant is a person who doesn't exercise his own will but rather submits it in order to please his master. He also demonstrates the importance of serving another without any assurance of reward.

## Biblical Characteristics Found in a Servant

Of all the biblical qualities ascribed to a servant, a number stand out clearly.

*A servant is humble.* He does not attract attention to himself. He stays in the background and does his work. Jesus taught that "a student is not above his teacher, nor a servant above his master" (Matthew 10:24). Paul said that the servant is to "gently instruct" those who oppose him (see 2 Timothy 2:25). Only a person who is truly humble before God can be gentle with those who oppose him.

*A servant is diligent.* He is active in doing his work; he is not slothful. Some of Jesus' strongest words were directed to this area of serving.

> Who then is the faithful and wise servant, whom the master has put in charge of the servants in his household to give them their food at the proper time? It will be good for that servant whose master finds him doing so

> when he returns. I tell you the truth, he will put him in charge of all his possessions (Matthew 24:45-47).

*A servant is busy serving.* The true servants of God are those who are busy about their business. Servants should serve, not do other things. This was the essence of Jesus' teaching on one occasion.

> Suppose one of you had a servant plowing or looking after the sheep. Would he say to the servant when he comes in from the field, "Come along now and sit down to eat"? Would he not rather say, "Prepare my supper, get yourself ready and wait on me while I eat and drink; after that you may eat and drink"? (Luke 17:7-8).

*A servant should be able to teach.* Primarily this means able to teach others to be servants. This is another characteristic that Paul urged as he challenged Timothy to serve others. "And the Lord's servant must not quarrel; instead, he must be kind to everyone, able to teach, not resentful" (2 Timothy 2:24). In countries where people work as servants, boys often come into a household as apprentices to learn how to be good servants. The older servants teach them everything they know about service to their masters.

*A servant is patient.* What a necessary virtue for all disciples. Paul urged Timothy, as a servant, to be patient (see 2 Timothy 2:24, KJV). The opposite of patience is being resentful with the circumstances that keep us from doing what we think ought to be done. One of the results of impatience is discouragement. A servant should do his work and not become discouraged when things don't go his way. The same is true when we as disciples spend time and work with others. As we serve them, we need patience so that we don't become discouraged.

*A servant is gentle.* That's an interesting trait to ascribe to a servant, but Scripture does so: "Those who oppose him he must gently instruct, in the hope that God will grant them repentance leading them to a knowledge of the truth" (2 Timothy 2:25). Paul instructed Timothy to be gentle with those of the opposition whom he would be instructing in the things of God. Roughness and rowdiness do not serve people.

*A servant is obedient.* Here's the heart of servanthood and the reason so many have problems with it. Paul wrote: "Slaves, obey your earthly masters with respect and fear, and with sincerity of heart, just as you would obey Christ. Obey them not only to win their favor when their eye is on you, but like slaves of Christ, doing the will of God from your heart" (Ephesians 6:5-6). One of the responsibilities of Christian leadership is to "teach slaves to be subject to their masters in everything, to try to please them, not to talk back to them" (Titus 2:9).

*A servant is dedicated.* When a servant commits himself to the one whom he serves, he does it with the totality of his heart. We have a beautiful example of that in Ittai the Gittite. David had been ousted in a palace coup by his son Absalom, and was now fleeing for his life. Ittai had gone with him, but David tried to convince him to return to King Absalom. "But Ittai replied to the king, 'As surely as the Lord lives, and as my lord the king lives, wherever my lord the king may be, whether it means life or death, there will your servant be' " (2 Samuel 15:21).

*A servant is watchful.* A servant needs to be alert to the needs his master might have and to the work that needs doing. Jesus spoke often about watchfulness. "Be dressed ready for service and keep your lamps burning, like men waiting for their master to return from a wedding banquet, so that when he comes and knocks they can immediately open the door for him" (Luke 12:35-36).

*A servant is faithful.* No matter what happens, a servant remains faithful to his master. That is the reputation David had in the days when King Saul was chasing him to kill him. Ahimelech the priest said of David to Saul, "Who of all your servants is as loyal as David, the king's son-in-law, captain of your bodyguard and highly respected in your household?" (1 Samuel 22:14)

*A servant does not talk back to his master.* A servant respects his master and does not talk back to him under any circumstances (see Titus 2:9). Harmony in the household enables the servant to do that which he is supposed to do—serve.

*A Christian disciple-servant is Spirit-filled.* The enabling power for Christian servanthood comes from the Holy Spirit of God. On the Day of Pentecost, Peter declared that Joel's prophecy was fulfilled and the age of the Holy Spirit had come. "This is what was spoken by the prophet Joel: . . . 'Even on my servants, both men and women, I will pour out my Spirit in those days' " (Acts 2:16,18). The power and filling of the Holy Spirit of God are necessary for real servanthood.

## Servanthood and Discipleship

Both by precept and example the Scriptures call on all of us who would be disciples of the Lord Jesus Christ to be his servants. When we act like servants, it is obvious to all.

When we were ministering in Charleston, South Carolina, Saturdays were workdays. As a part of their training program, the men to whom we were ministering would come to the house on Saturdays to do some work.

One of the problems we had was the presence of thirty-three pine trees on our property. There were pine needles everywhere. They would fall on the roof and plug up the drain pipes; or they would rot on the roof, causing holes, and then the roof leaked.

One Saturday six of the men climbed onto my roof and cleaned off the pine needles. My neighbor across the street saw what was going on, came over and asked, "Where do you get all these people to do your work?" When I told him they were part of my ministry, he went away shaking his head. The men who had cleaned my roof got the ladder out again, climbed up on the neighbor's roof, and cleaned up all his needles. Now that's servanthood. That incident opened my neighbor's heart to the gospel like nothing else had before.

Servanthood is intensely practical. It works in everyday life. Some thirty people would come to our house on Monday nights for Bible study. After the study was over, some of these men and women would straighten up the furniture and put the house back in order. They would also wash the cups and plates, and then put them away. These people were servants.

I'll always remember three young women that we had the privilege of ministering to. After they became Christians, they would ask my wife, "Norma, what do you want me to do? Is there any ironing that needs to be done? What do you need done around the house?" We never asked them to do anything; they just wanted to serve us and the Lord. They were real servants. Today all three of them continue to be active in the Lord's work on the mission field, in Navigator ministries, and in the home and community.

Many people have the doctrines of Scripture down pat, but are unfamiliar with the techniques of service.

Others are doing Bible study and memorizing Scripture, but are not willing to spend time in serving. This is one of the greatest weaknesses in Christendom today. The servants are few while the needs and opportunities are many.

## How We Can Be Servants

Servanthood is intensely practical and should be the warp and woof of each disciple's life. Here are some suggestions on how we can be servants of Jesus Christ and others.

### *Be Willing to Do Menial Tasks*

This is one of the hardest things to teach to a person in Western society today. Many think that menial tasks are below them. Note this incident in the life of the Apostle Paul:

> Once safely on shore, we found out that the island was called Malta. The islanders showed us unusual kindness. They built a fire and welcomed us all because it was raining and cold. Paul gathered a pile of brushwood and, as he put it on the fire, a viper, driven out by the heat, fastened itself on his hand (Acts 28:1-3).

The great Apostle Paul gathered firewood on a cold, rainy day right after a traumatic shipwreck. He could just as easily have rested and let the kind islanders do all the work. But Paul was a servant and demonstrated it vividly even at the expense of being bitten by a snake. Possibly that opened up an opportunity to proclaim the gospel. We must be willing to do menial tasks.

In our discipleship training at Glen Eyrie we often assign men and women who first come there to menial tasks. It is not uncommon to find a Ph.D. working on the lawn crew or a graduate engineer washing dishes. Women who are in business make beds and nurses wait on tables. It is an excellent opportunity for these well-educated and successful people to learn servanthood at the practical level.

*Be Available*

One of the characteristics of servants in a household is that they must be available when the master calls them. The Christian servant must also be available—to God and to those it is his ministry to serve. We must not be like those who made all kinds of excuses when Jesus called them to follow him.

> He said to another man, "Follow me."
>
> But the man replied, "Lord, first let me go and bury my father."
>
> Jesus said to him, "Let the dead bury their own dead, but you go and proclaim the kingdom of God."
>
> Still another said, "I will follow you, Lord; but first let me go back and say good-by to my family."
>
> Jesus replied,"No one who puts his hand to the plow and looks back is fit for service in the kingdom of God" (Luke 9:59-62).

*Be Observant*

A servant must be alert to the needs of others. The psalmist wrote, "As the eyes of slaves look to the hand of their master, as the eyes of a maid look to the hand of her mistress, so our eyes look to the Lord our God, till he shows us his mercy" (Psalm 123:2). The needs of guests in a Hebrew household were communicated to the servants by hand signals, so it was the responsibility of those serving to watch the hands of the master and mistress.

When Dawson Trotman was president of The Navigators, he lived in a lovely, large home on the grounds of Glen Eyrie. The home had a large dining room and a table that seated about eighteen people. The Trotmans entertained often, and I was always amazed at how efficiently the girls who were serving met our needs without anyone saying a word. I was puzzled by this and finally asked Lila Trotman about it. She said it was all based on Psalm 123:2. The girls had been taught to observe the hand signals that Daws or Lila made signifying a need a guest might have.

When I was in training to become a Navigator representative, I learned it shouldn't always be necessary to be told to do jobs that needed to be done. If you saw that one of the knobs on a cabinet was loose, you got a screwdriver and tightened it. If you noticed that the kids had been pushing out the back porch screen, you repaired it. A servant should take the initiative and do whatever has to be done. That's practical servanthood.

On one occasion I was traveling with Ron York, a Navigator representative. We stopped at a service station for some gas. When Ron came out of the restroom, he asked the station manager for some cleanser and paper towels. Then he went back and cleaned the bathroom, which was filthy. We had been trained to leave a bathroom cleaner than when we went into it. A public bathroom? Yes, because the principle of servanthood applies there as well.

*Do More Than You Are Asked to Do*

Western society is governed by clock-watching. People do just what they are asked to do, nothing more. If they are asked to do a little more than their job description calls for, they want overtime or other compensation. A true servant does what he is supposed to do, and more.

## THE RESULTS OF BEING A TRUE SERVANT

What happens in a person's life when he manifests the characteristics of servanthood? The Bible does have something to say about these "rewards."

The servant may experience the service of his master.

> It will be good for those servants whose master finds them watching when he comes. I tell you the truth, he will dress himself to serve, will have them recline at the table and will come and wait on them. It will be good for those servants whose master finds them ready, even if he comes in the second or third watch of the night (Luke 12:37-38).

The servant who is faithful in all his responsibilities will be recognized by the master whom he so faithfully serves. The master of such a man will say, "Well done, good and faithful servant! You have been faithful with a few things; I will put you in charge of many things. Come and share your master's happiness!" (Matthew 25:21).

God gives his servants wisdom for the responsibilities committed to them. When Solomon became king, he prayed:

> Your servant is here among the people you have chosen, a great people, too numerous to count or number. So give your servant a discerning heart to govern your people and to distinguish between right and wrong. For who is able to govern this great people of yours? (1 Kings 3:8-9)

God granted his request for wisdom, and Solomon became one of the wisest men who ever lived.

Honor from God comes to the faithful servant of the Lord. Jesus said, "Whoever serves me must follow me; and where I am, my servant also will be. My Father will honor the one who serves me" (John 12:26).

* * *

You cannot be a true disciple of Jesus Christ unless you have a servant heart.

NOTES: 1. LeRoy Eims, *Be the Leader You Were Meant to Be* (Wheaton, Illinois: Victor Books, 1975), p. 40.

# CHAPTER 11 THE MINISTRY OF GIVING

*A disciple gives regularly and honors God with his finances.*

One of the great privileges that we have in our Christian life is giving to God's work. Giving is a lordship decision ultimately, in which we turn over control of our money to Christ. Giving also is an evidence of our gratitude for what he has done for us in redemption.

## Giving Is an Investment in Heaven

There is no way we can take the material things or other accomplishments of this world into the spiritual realm. Or is there? Jesus said in the Sermon on the Mount: "Do not store up for yourselves treasures on earth, where moth and rust destroy, and where thieves break in and steal. But store up for yourselves treasures in heaven, where moth and rust do not destroy, and where thieves do not break in and steal" (Matthew 6:19-20).

Jesus said that we invest our treasures in heaven by giving to the poor of this world. "Jesus looked at him [the rich young man] and loved him. 'One thing you lack,' he said. 'Go, sell everything you have and give to the poor, and you will have treasure in heaven. Then come, follow me' " (Mark 10:21). This man had so much, yet he lacked treasure in heaven.

Paul wrote to a very generous church and said, "Not that I am looking for a gift, but I am looking for what may be credited to your account" (Philippians 4:17). The context of this statement tells of the generosity of the Philippians in supporting Paul, in sharing with him out of their poverty, and in sending him aid when he had needs. Whatever we give will be credited to our spiritual account.

God will not forget our genuine works of love. We may not be recognized by men in this world, nor receive monetary rewards, but God will never forget what we have done for him. "God is not unjust; he will not forget your work and the love you have shown him as you have helped his people and continue to help them" (Hebrews 6:10). The man who fears the Lord "has scattered abroad his gifts to the poor, his righteousness endures for ever" (Psalm 112:9). This is not our righteousness in terms of sin, but our acting rightly in terms of giving. Treasures in heaven result from helping the people of God. This principle is supported by Solomon. "He who is kind to the poor lends to the Lord, and he will reward him for what he has done" (Proverbs 19:17).

## The Blessings of Giving

Giving always brings with it tremendous blessings. Jesus said, "It is more blessed to give than to receive" (Acts

20:35). When we give to others, we receive a double blessing. We are blessed because we have given and we are blessed through those to whom we have given.

The people of God rejoice when there has been generous giving. The giver rejoices and the recipients rejoice. God told David that he was to gather materials for building the temple of the Lord. David gave his own treasures. He also shared the need with the whole nation and the people gladly began giving. "The people rejoiced at the willing response of their leaders, for they had given freely and wholeheartedly to the Lord. David the king also rejoiced greatly" (1 Chronicles 29:9).

We once had a project at one of our military conferences overseas. The plan was to raise $4,025 for the servicemen's ministries in the Orient. We shared the need with the 175 men and took a collection.

We began counting the money and quickly passed $4,000. We ended up wih nearly $15,000. Jim Downing was our speaker, so we went to him and asked, "Jim, what are we going to do with all this extra money?" Jim at that time was in charge of all our Navigator servicemen's work around the world and knew of other needs elsewhere. So he shared some of those needs with us. We prayed about them, and designated the rest of the funds for those needs.

Then we shared with the men at the conference what God had done through them. We told them God had laid these other projects on our hearts. There was tremendous excitement at the conference and much rejoicing by all who were there. God received all the glory for what he had done through the men who had given so generously.

*God Will Supply Our Needs*

Whatever our needs may be—spiritual, physical, financial—God promises to meet them. Paul thanked one church for their ample gifts and concluded with the assurance that "my God will meet all your needs according to his glorious riches in Christ Jesus" (Philippians 4:19). The implication is that if we give of our substance, God will supply all our needs.

One of the reasons some Christians continue to be plagued with financial troubles is because of their giving program. If a Christian is not honoring God with his income, he will experience financial difficulties.

In my previous book, *Essentials of New Life,* I told of the provision of God for our financial needs when we were going overseas. In a marvelous way God caused us to meet a couple who became burdened for our needs. They presented our need to a foundation in their hometown, and sold some cattle. The profit from the sale of the cattle plus the foundation money came to *exactly* the additional amount we needed to travel to Japan—$623.20. On our way home from Japan, we needed transportation money for ourselves and our household goods. As we prayed about it, the Lord led twenty-three people to send in the entire amount! God does keep his promise to meet the needs of his people.

Approaching one Christmas season we discovered we were in debt to the amount of $700 and wanted to be out of it by the new year. We prayed about it but did not make our needs known. Some days before Christmas a letter came from a couple we had ministered to in another city. Enclosed was a check for $200. That same day I opened some of the Christmas cards we had received and found checks for $60, $50, and $50. That evening a couple came over just bubbling with excitement. The man told us, "God has really blessed us this year. I was just paid a tremendous unexpected bonus by my company and want to share it with you because of your ministry to us." He sat down and wrote us a check for $1,000. God answered our prayer, met our needs, and provided extra money for Christmas as well.

*God Gives as We Have Given*

God desires to give us blessings beyond simply meeting our needs. Jesus told his disciples: "Give, and it will be given to you. A good measure, pressed down, shaken together and running over, will be poured into your lap. For with the measure you use, it will be measured to you" (Luke 6:38). Paul expressed the same idea when he stated that "whoever sows sparingly will also reap sparingly, and whoever sows generously will also reap generously" (2 Corinthians 9:6). We cannot determine the form God's blessing will take, but we do determine the quantity by how much we have given.

*God Will Provide Abundantly*

On a number of occasions God indicated clearly that he cannot be outgiven. He gives back far more than is ever given to him. In fact, he pours it out on the generous giver. The prophet recorded God's words in the Old Testament: "Bring the whole tithe into the storehouse, that there may be food in my house. Test me in this, . . .and see if I will not throw open the floodgates of heaven and pour out so much blessing that you will not have room enough for it" (Malachi 3:10).

Solomon referred more than once to God's abundant supply. "One man gives freely, yet gains even more; another withholds unduly, but comes to poverty. A generous man will prosper; he who refreshes others will himself be refreshed" (Proverbs 11:24-25). In the *King James Version* the phrase *will prosper* is translated "shall be made fat," a vivid picture of God's blessing on liberality. Earlier Solomon had advised God's people to "honor the Lord with your wealth, with the firstfruits of all your crops; then your barns will be filled to overflowing, and your vats will brim over with new wine" (Proverbs 3:9-10). In our day and age this simply means that God will provide more than we need, even as he did in the agricultural society of ancient Israel.

One man who vividly demonstrates the grace of giving is Harvey Oslund, a Navigator representative. I have never met anyone who gives as much as he does. The people who come out of his ministry are great givers as well. Harvey is not only a powerful preacher on this topic, but he demonstrates it clearly in his own life. When we visit him, he won't allow us to pay for anything. When he comes to our area, he still wants to pay for everything. We have to tell him to give us the opportunity and privilege to be generous in return.

Those of us who had the privilege of going through Navigator training with Dawson Trotman remember him as a man of tremendous generosity. If you admired a shirt or tie he was wearing, he'd take it off and give it to you. That's the kind of man he was. Early in his Christian life he had discovered the grace of giving. He died giving his life for another.

We may also receive blessings of another kind. Because the early Church gave so freely to one another, they experienced unity, love, gladness, singleness of heart, praise, and growth in numbers (see Acts 2:44-47).

## How Should We Give?

We want to look at nine adjectives or descriptive phrases telling how we are to give to the Lord and to his work.

1. We are to give *willingly and cheerfully.* Giving is never to be done with a grudging attitude or as the result of pressure. We have already seen that in the days of David the people "had given freely and whole-heartedly to the Lord" (1 Chronicles 29:9). In his prayer later on, David added: "I know, my God, that you test the heart and are pleased with integrity. All these things have I given willingly and with honest intent. And now I have seen with joy how willingly your people who are here have given to you" (1 Chronicles 29:17).

Paul taught this principle in the New Testament. "For if the willingness is there, the gift is acceptable according to what one has, not according to what he does not have" (2 Corinthians 8:12). He goes on to say that "each man should give what he has decided in his heart to give, not reluctantly or under compulsion, for God loves a cheerful giver" (2 Corinthians 9:7).

2. We are to give *joyfully.* We should consider giving such a privilege that joy should well up in our hearts because we are able to do so. The church at Philippi was known for its joyful giving. "And now, brothers, we want you to know about the grace that God has given the Macedonian churches [Philippi among them]. Out of the most severe trial, their overflowing joy and their extreme poverty welled up in rich generosity" (2 Corinthians 8:1-2).

3. We are to give *thoughtfully.* Only after prayer should we decide what to give and to whom we should give it. That's what Paul meant when he said, "Each man should give what he has decided in his heart to give, not reluctantly or under compulsion" (2 Corinthians 9:7).

4. We are to give *with a perfect heart.* There must be no hidden or mixed motives in our giving, particularly the motive of seeking reward. David acknowledged to God in

prayer that he had given "with honest intent" (1 Chronicles 29:17).

5. We are to give *mercifully.* We give because we are merciful to those in need. That was the attitude of the psalmist when he wrote, "The wicked borrows, and cannot pay back, but the righteous is generous and gives" (Psalm 37:21, RSV).

6. We are to give *unselfishly.* Paul urged his readers to "share with God's people who are in need" (Romans 12:13). He explained this to the Corinthians:

> Our desire is not that others might be relieved while you are hard pressed, but that there might be equality. At the present time your plenty will supply what they need, so that in turn their plenty will supply what you need. Then there will be equality, as it is written: "He that gathered much did not have too much, and he that gathered little did not have too little" (2 Corinthians 8:13-15).

7. We are to give *generously.* In many passages which we have looked at already, the Bible urges generosity. When Paul was talking about spiritual gifts, he said of giving, "If it is contributing to the needs of others, let him give generously" (Romans 12:8).

8. We are to give *sacrificially.* The Macedonian churches were known for their sacrificial giving (see 2 Corinthians 8:2-3). The most beautiful example of that kind of giving is the observation of Jesus one day in the temple.

> As he looked up, Jesus saw the rich putting their gifts into the temple treasury. He also saw a poor widow put in two very small copper coins. "I tell you the truth," he said, "this poor widow has put in more than all the

others. All these people gave their gifts out of their wealth; but she out of her poverty put in all she had to live on" (Luke 21:1-4).

9. We are to give *secretly.* This does not necessarily mean anonymously, but it does mean that we do not flaunt our giving before others. Jesus taught this in the Sermon on the Mount:

> Be careful not to do your "acts of righteousness" before men, to be seen by them. If you do, you will have no reward from your Father in heaven. . . .But when you give to the needy, do not let your left hand know what your right hand is doing, so that your giving may be in secret. Then your Father, who sees what is done in secret, will reward you (Matthew 6:1, 3-4).

When I was in training at the Navigator headquarters in the 1950s, we were paid $30 a month plus room and board. As long as we had no outstanding debts, we could get through a month on that salary, and sometimes there would be some money left over. I had a burden to give it back to The Navigators, so at the end of the month I would go over to the office and empty out my pockets. I remember doing that two or three times and then the Lord convicted me about doing it so openly. So I put my left-over money into an envelope and sent it over through the interoffice mail so that no credit would come to Francis Cosgrove from men.

## To Whom Should We Give?

God wants us to give to the needy. James wrote, "Suppose

a brother or sister is without clothes and daily food. If one of you says to him, 'Go, I wish you well; keep warm and well fed,' but does nothing about his physical needs, what good is it?" (James 2:15-16)

When I lived in the Navigator home in Oakland, California, I was studying the book of James and came to this passage. Through my study I was convicted about giving to the needs of one of the other men in the home. He was in financial straits while I had money in my savings account. So I withdrew the money and gave it to him.

Paul exhorted the former thief, a person who had now come to Christ, to make giving to the needy an integral part of his life. "He who has been stealing must steal no longer, but must work, doing something useful with his own hands, that he may have something to share with those in need" (Ephesians 4:28).

The needy are all around us, including in our churches. When I was serving at Coral Ridge, the ministerial staff had access to a deacon's fund. If I discovered that someone in the church had a need, I was authorized to put in a request for money from the fund to meet those needs. Every church should have a plan for meeting physical needs.

Throughout Scripture the people of God are called on to support those who work for the Lord full-time. In the Old Testament nation of Israel, the people were reminded that they had to suppport the Levites. They were men of the tribe of Levi who were serving the Lord in the tabernacle and as instructors of the Law. Moses wrote, "Be careful not to neglect the Levites as long as you live in your land" (Deuteronomy 12:19). The people were responsible to take care of the needs of these religious workers.

We are to help those who are ministering out of our own means. We find a beautiful example of that in the gospels as Jesus was proclaiming the good news. The Twelve were traveling with him, as were some women who had been cured of evil spirits and diseases. "These women were helping to support them out of their own means" (Luke 8:3).

We are to support those who instruct us. Paul told the Galatians, "The man under Christian instruction should be willing to contribute toward the livelihood of his teacher" (Galatians 6:6, PH).

Epaphroditus is an example of a person supporting and ministering to another. Paul wrote of him, "But I think it is necessary to send back to you Epaphroditus, my brother, fellow worker and fellow soldier, who is also your messenger, whom you sent to take care of my needs" (Philippians 2:25). He ministered to Paul's needs in many ways.

Onesiphorus was another man who ministered to Paul. "May the Lord show mercy to the household of Onesiphorus, because he often refreshed me and was not ashamed of my chains. On the contrary, when he was in Rome, he searched hard for me until he found me. . . .You know very well in how many ways he helped me in Ephesus" (2 Timothy 1:16-18).

The starting point in our giving must be the local church in which we are being ministered to with the word of God. It is up to you to divide your giving between the various funds in the church budget.

God's work is also done through various Christian organizations. These organizations may have ministered to us in some way. If so, we are also responsible to give to their support. Because Evangelism Explosion has meant so much in the lives of many people in Coral Ridge Presbyterian Church, they give to that organization. This is giving beyond the 10 percent responsibility to the local church. My own organization, The Navigators, has been of help to countless people around the world and many of those people give to its ministry. This is also true of foreign missions organizations.

Each of these organizations has needs for support of individuals, administration, and special projects such as buildings and equipment. We give to individuals because they are our friends or have ministered in our life, or because we want to be involved in the outreach of the gospel in other parts of the world. We give to administrative support because organizations need to function well behind the lines as well as in the field. We give to special projects to increase an organization's effectiveness.

## Practical Instructions on Giving

Here are some practical things you can do to begin or to strengthen your giving.

### *Start with 11 Percent*

We have already considered the words of God through the Prophet Malachi about giving according to the amount God has prospered us (see Malachi 3:10). The best way to give is by using a percentage. I have always suggested to men with whom I have worked that they begin with 11 percent of their gross income. Of that portion, 10 percent is the obedience gift, and 1 percent is the love gift. If one man earns $100 a week, he would start out by giving $11, while the man who makes $500 a week would give $55. We should raise that proportion as God prospers and leads us to give.

When I was in the Navy I was able to give a substantial proportion of my income for the work of the Lord. As a single man with no responsibilities or indebtedness, I could trust God for everything. I knew that it was probably the only time in my life that I would ever be able to give in such a way. When I got married, Norma and I again began with 15 percent and have raised it as the Lord has prospered and led us.

*Give to the Lord First*

The Bible's presentation of giving is that we should give to the Lord first, as Paul suggested. "On the first day of every week, each one of you should set aside a sum of money in keeping with his income, saving it up, so that when I come no collections will have to be made" (1 Corinthians 16:2).

*Give Consistently*

This does not mean that we have to give every week, but we are to be regular in our giving. If you are paid twice a month, you might want to give twice a month; if you have structured your giving at the end of the month, give at the end of the month. The main point is to be consistent in your giving. This is what Paul taught the Corinthians in the passage above.

*Make Extra Gifts*

Special needs in an individual's life, in the church, or in an organization will arise periodically, and it is our privilege to give extra gifts to meet those needs. This is part of our opportunity to be generous with what the Lord has prospered us. Remember, God can never be outgiven!

*Honor Your Pledges*

When you make a commitment or pledge, be sure that you can fulfill it. Remember Jesus' words of instruction:

"Simply let your 'Yes' be 'Yes,' and your 'No,' 'No' " (Matthew 5:37). Determine with God's help what you can do. Never make a pledge that would take money away from your local church commitment.

If the level of your income falls and you are unable to meet your commitments on a regular basis, be sure to notify the church, organization, or individual. It is simply a courtesy to them and helps them in their planning and raising of further support. I know how I have appreciated being notified by people when they had to cut down or were not able to give to my support any longer.

* * *

Giving is a privilege and an honor for Christian disciples. According to the teachings of God's Word, he will bless what we give joyfully and ungrudgingly to him and his workers. We are storing up treasure in heaven which will be a part of that great reward when we stand before Jesus Christ.

# CHAPTER 12
# THE FRUIT OF THE SPIRIT

*A disciple demonstrates the fruit of the Spirit by an attractive relationship with Christ and his fellowman.*

The visible life of a disciple must show clearly that he is a follower of Jesus Christ. Others should be able to see in his life the fruit of the Holy Spirit of God. In practice a disciple must live out the reality of what Paul talks about: "But the fruit of the Spirit is love, joy, peace, patience, kindness, goodness, faithfulness, gentleness and self-control. Against such things there is no law" (Galatians 5:22-23).

## What Is the Fruit of the Spirit?

Matthew Henry offers some comments to increase our understanding of the fruit produced by the Holy Spirit:

> He [Paul] particularly recommends to us, *love,* to God especially, and to one another for his sake,—*joy,* by which may be understood cheerfulness in conversation

> with our friends, or rather a constant delight in God,—*peace*, with God and conscience, or a peaceableness of temper and behavior toward others,—*longsuffering*, patience to defer anger, and a contentedness to bear injuries,—*gentleness*, such a sweetness of temper, and especially towards our inferiors, as disposes us to be affable and courteous, and easy to be entreated when any have wronged us,—*goodness* (kindness, beneficence), which shows itself in a readiness to do good to all as we have opportunity,—*faith*, fidelity, justice, and honesty, in what we profess and promise to others,—*meekness*, wherewith to govern our passions and resentments, so as not to be easily provoked, and, when we are so, to be soon pacified,—and *temperance*, in meat and drink, and other enjoyments of life, so as not to be excessive and immoderate in the use of them. Concerning these things, or those in whom these fruits of the Spirit are found, the Apostle says, *There is no law against them*, to condemn and punish them.[1]

When we count the fruit of the Spirit Paul lists for the Galatians, we discover that there are nine. The number nine in Scripture is not very common, but it does appear at times and has some significance. Scholars believe that this number, which is the numerical result of 3 x 3, in its symbolic usage has the meaning of finality, or completion.

## The Fruit of the Spirit Is Visible

The fruit Paul is listing to the Galatians is specifically the fruit of the Holy Spirit. When we receive Jesus Christ as our personal Savior and Lord, we are baptized by the Holy Spirit; he takes up residence in our heart and we become his temple. The evidence that he is within us is through the fruit.

This brings us to an important question: Is the fruit of the Spirit visible in the life of every believer? We know it should be, but many times it isn't. On the other hand, there are men and women who beautifully demonstrate the fruit of the Spirit.

When I first arrived in Fort Lauderdale, I was quickly attracted to Jim Kennedy. I wanted to follow him because he so vividly demonstrated in his life a depth of relationship and an attractive daily walk with Jesus Christ. This is not to idolize him, but to say that God uses the lives of others to deepen our own.

*The Analogy of Fruit*

When Paul spoke of fruit, he used an agricultural analogy that would be easily understood. Fruit is the desired product of sowing seed. When the farmer plants his seeds, he anticipates the fruit of that crop. Between the planting and the harvesting, the field must be carefully tended to produce the best possible fruit. The soil around the crop must be weeded and requires continual care so that it might bear the most fruit. In an orchard, the trees are pruned regularly. Finally comes the harvest and the fruit is reaped and used or sold.

Fruit is the evidence of life. If there was no life in the seed, there would be no fruit. Fruit is the result of reaching maturity, the completion of one life cycle and the beginning of another. The seed produces fruit, and out of the fruit come more seeds for next year's season. In this process we see multiplication of seed and fruit.

Fruit in the spiritual realm is the result of a right relationship with Jesus Christ. It is evidence of the fact that his Holy Spirit lives in us. The spiritual process of a seed being planted, growing, being pruned, and reaching maturity must produce fruit. We are known by the fruit we produce. Jesus said, "Thus, by their fruit you will recognize them" (Matthew 7:20). The evidence that we belong to Jesus is in the fruit that we produce and others see.

## The Fruit of the Spirit Is Attractive

Well developed fruit is attractive. The "amber waves of grain" and full-fruited orchards attract our attention. It is a beautiful sight to see trees with ripening fruit, whether they be apple, pear, orange, or plum. We know that the fruit in the garden of Eden was attractive, for Eve "saw that the fruit of the tree was good for food and pleasing to the eye" (Genesis 3:6).

### *We Must Walk with God*

People will respond to an attractive life when they see it. We all know fellow Christians whose lives we would like to emulate. All we have to do is look around in our church, in Christian organizations, in our job, and in society to find men and women who are living attractive Christian lives. We can't help but be challenged by them. We want to be like them. But we should follow them only as they are following Jesus Christ.

Many biographies of Christians today and throughout church history present us with attractive lives. As we read the records of their lives and see the godliness that was visible in their walk with Jesus, we want to be like them and like him.

We are exhorted in Scripture to lead attractive lives. The Apostle Paul wrote to a church which was having some difficulties in this area: "Follow my example, as I follow the example of Christ" (1 Corinthians 11:1). Paul followed the example of the most attractive life the world has seen. In another letter Paul wrote, "Whatever you have learned or received or heard from me, or seen in me—put it into practice" (Philippians 4:9). Paul had an attractive relationship with Jesus Christ which was visible, as evidenced by the crowds that followed him.

We are also exhorted to have attractive lives in ways that do not depend on an example. The Apostle Peter tells us to "grow in the grace and knowledge of our Lord and Savior Jesus Christ" (2 Peter 3:18). In his earlier letter he had asked:

> But how is it to your credit if you receive a beating for doing wrong and endure it? But if you suffer for doing good and you endure it, this is commendable before God. To this you were called, because Christ suffered for you, leaving you an example, that you should follow in his steps (1 Peter 2:20-21).

The Apostle Paul challenged our thinking when he pointed out that "those God foreknew he also predestined to be conformed to the likeness of his Son" (Romans 8:29). Our destiny is that we be conformed to the likeness of Jesus Christ. That will be a tremendous attraction to men. In contrast to those who live in sin, Paul tells us to "clothe yourselves with the Lord Jesus Christ, and do not think about how to gratify the desires of the sinful nature" (Romans 13:14).

*We Should Attract Unbelievers*

No matter how reluctant they are to admit it, unbelievers are attracted to Christians who follow Jesus This was the case when the apostles Peter and John were brought before the Sanhedrin, the ruling body of the Jews. Even the unsaved members of this ecclesiastical body recognized unusual courage and knew that these men had been with Jesus. Peter and John were bearing fruit to that fact, and that was attractive even to the Sanhedrin.

The life of Jesus Christ in a new believer will be highly visible, and it will be attractive. This should happen every time God redeems a person to himself. I remember the privilege of leading a teenage girl to Christ. Kim Roberts was president of the student council in her high school. She had been elected Hurricane Queen and reigned over all the fall activities. After she became a Christian, Kim received training in evangelism at Coral Ridge and led scores of her high school friends to the Savior. Many of them were attracted by the positive changes in her life. The implanted Christ became visible in her life.

## The Fruit of the Spirit Is Fragile

My Evangelism Explosion team would often recognize immediately that the person we were calling on was a Christian. On one occasion an elderly woman opened the door and greeted us so kindly that we thought she was a Christian. Our further conversation with her bore out our first impression. The way she treated us made the fruit of the Spirit obvious in her.

Unfortunately, however, not all Christians demonstrate the fruit of the Spirit. Their relationship with Jesus Christ and the Holy Spirit is not as it should be.

### *Sin Is in Control*

A Christian may be trusting Christ for his salvation, but he is living in sin, not under the control of the Holy

Spirit. The presence of sin in a life snuffs out evidence that the Holy Spirit is there. Paul warned clearly, "Do not grieve the Holy Spirit of God, with whom you were sealed for the day of redemption" (Ephesians 4:30).

James warned that it is impossible for the person who claims to be a Christian but is living in sin to manifest the fruit of the Holy Spirit of God. He was speaking about the use of their tongues, but the same truth applies to every aspect of a Christian's life.

> With the tongue we praise our Lord and Father, and with it we curse men, who have been made in God's likeness. Out of the same mouth come praise and cursing. My brothers, this should not be. Can both fresh water and salt water flow from the same spring? My brothers, can a fig tree bear olives, or a grapevine bear figs? Neither can a salt spring produce fresh water (James 3:9-12).

*Jesus Christ Is Not Lord*

God will not manifest himself through the Holy Spirit in the life of a person who is rebellious against his authority and still has self on the throne of his life. God simply won't show his presence in a person who wants to go his own way. "For rebellion is like the sin of divination, and arrogance like the evil of idolatry" (1 Samuel 15:23). The key issue is lordship; the Christian is not allowing Jesus Christ to be Lord of his life.

Christians who have not submitted to Jesus' lordship are not his disciples. They may have received him as Savior, but not as Lord. That commitment to his lordship starts a person on the road to being his disciple. A disciple has a dynamic relationship with God, demonstrating attractively the fruit of the Spirit.

## How We Can Develop Fruit in Our Life

In our own strength alone, we cannot develop the fruit of the Spirit in our life. It comes only in partnership with the indwelling Holy Spirit. Our responsibility is to recognize our need in certain areas of our life. If we give ourself to walking in the Spirit, he will produce the needed fruit in us. We must give complete control of our body, mind, and soul to Christ, and let him demonstrate his power in and through us.

The missing link in many Christians' lives is diligence in developing this fruit. The Apostle Peter had this to say about our responsibility:

> For this very reason, make every effort to add to your faith goodness; and to goodness, knowledge; and to knowledge, self-control; and to self-control, perseverance; and to perseverance, godliness; and to godliness, brotherly kindness; and to brotherly kindness, love. For if you possess these qualities in increasing measure, they will keep you from being ineffective and unproductive in your knowledge of our Lord Jesus Christ (2 Peter 1:5-8).

We are to "make every effort!" If we have problems with self-control, for example, then it is our responsibility to learn to control ourself. The Holy Spirit will provide the strength we lack. The same is true with the other qualities.

When I was in Japan, I discovered a fruit that is the most delicious of any I have tasted throughout the world. The Japanese name for it means "20th century pear." It is a cross between an apple and a pear. I was curious about how this marvelous fruit was grown, so I went out into the country to find out.

I discovered that the farmers use a laborious process

to guarantee the success of these pears. The trees are carefully pruned before they begin the flowering process in the spring. As soon as the flowers are gone and the fruit begins to appear, the workers go to each tree and tie a small brown bag around each fruit. Periodically they will take a bag off to see how the tree and the crop are doing. The bags remain there till the harvest to protect the fruit from the elements, birds, bugs, and other detrimental factors. A great deal of work and care is necessary to produce this quality of fruit.

* * *

The fruit of the Spirit should be so obvious in your life, and so attractive to men, that they desire to know how such fruit was produced. Just as in the case of the Japanese pears, the fruit of the Spirit will reach maturity if it receives careful attention and is protected from harmful conditions

## Conclusion

This book was written with you in mind, you who want to be a disciple and make other disciples. Disciplemaking begins with you. You have to be a disciple before you can make another disciple. There will be struggles and difficulties. You will discover it is costly. The Holy Spirit will carry on his pruning process, with the end result that you become more like Christ.

Your personal desire to become a man of God or a woman of God must have priority, for it is from this platform of living example that you can launch out to reach and train others. In fact, men and women will come to you seeking your spiritual assistance. The vitality of your relationship to Christ is very important in a disciplemaking ministry.

In the ministry of disciplemaking, we need to realize we have an enemy—Satan. He will seek to discourage our spirit by telling us, "You'll never make any disciples." If I had listened to that at the beginning, in the midst of failures and lack of skill, I would have quit long ago.

Claim promises for your disciplemaking ministry from God's word. How can you help but be encouraged by promises such as those in Isaiah 43:4-6:

> Since you are precious and honored in my sight, and because I love you, I will give men in exchange for you, and people in exchange for your life. Do not be afraid, for I am with you; I will bring your children from the east and gather you from the west. I will say to the north, "Give them up!" and to the south, "Do not hold them back." Bring my sons from afar and my daughters from the ends of the earth.

Perhaps the greatest motivation for anyone to make disciples is the example of others. Associate with those who have this on their heart.

May I also remind you that we learn to do by doing. That principle certainly applies to disciplemaking. You learn how to become proficient in disciplemaking by making disciples. You will make mistakes, and you'll loose some of those you're working with to other interest (see Mark 4:19). But eventually you will hit a winner. God will multiply your ministry and use you to "raise up the foun dations of many generations" (Isaiah 58:12, KJV).

To minimize failure and discouragement, use 2 Timothy 2:2 as a guide in looking for potential disciples.

Those who will eventually reproduce must be "reliable men who will also be qualified to teach others." If you only have a person who is reliable, you'll never reproduce. He must be able to teach others.

Start today by asking God to bring a person into your life to disciple, and begin to look for that person. You won't be making disciples tomorrow if you don't get started today.

My prayer is that God will make you a strong disciplemaker.

---

NOTES: 1. Matthew Henry, *Matthew Henry's Commentary On the Whole Bible*, 6 vols. (Old Tappan, New Jersey: Fleming H. Revell Company, n.d.), 6· n.p.

# SCRIPTURE INDEX